# THE DIVINE PRAISES

## Addresses to Holy Name Societies

---

### I. INTRODUCTORY

"Thou shalt not take the name of the Lord thy God in vain"

*SYNOPSIS.—Introductory—Sin inherently an offense against God. Its consequences as a free act to be incurred and faced at one's peril. Though all sins essentially evil, yet those directly against God, cursing, perjury, blasphemy, involve special malice. Blasphemy offense against civil law punishable by death. Socrates; Our Lord. Humblest citizens have protection against defamers of their good name and character· God alone undefended Abuse of Holy Name.*
*I. Society formed in vindication and defense of Holy Name, and to uphold right of God generally. Individual efforts against deeply rooted evils powerless Combination vital. Joint action alone tells, else we are as single drops of water or detached rays of light Leagues exist against all public abuses. What greater or more crying public evil than abuse of God's name?*
*II. Object of society twofold; (a) war against abuse and (b) promotion of good use of Holy Name. (a) Abuse of God's name universal amongst all ranks, in press, platform and even pulpit Society of Holy Name to promote observance of Second Commandment (b) But main object use of Holy Name in true piety, prayer and praise. Ignoring God a form of blasphemy, in part both of nation and individual. World is God's, therefore should His praise be in all life. Recital of Divine Praises ordered by Pope Leo XIII. Groundwork of present course We have all to bear testimony to Christ-God. One means is recital of Divine Praise. Name of ruler prominent in every state on coins, in law and all branches of public life Name of God should be equally prominent in His Kingdom, the Church. How Society of Holy Name may contribute to promote this great end. Exhortation to practise reverence and respect for Holy Name.*

Broadly speaking, the essence of sin lies in the conflict of the human will with the Divine. It is the free act of a creature refusing to obey God, speaking through conscience and law. Sin, therefore, implies more than a mere breach of social regulations, or the failure to live up to one's ideal. It is the deliberate rupture of a tie, that under the name of duty, binds man to God—the creature to the Creator. "If thou dost ill . . . shall not sin forthwith be present at the door," but, "thou shalt have dominion over it" (Gen. iv, 7).

Other views of sin, I know, are held to-day, and theories framed to elude its consequences; but we, who, in this matter, are "taught of God," need not concern ourselves with the phantom theologies of the hour, voiced by men, "wise in their own conceits." The groundwork of Christian ethics is that sin is *inherently,* and *essentially,* evil, and as such, a thing to be done at one's peril. Forgiven it may be; excused, never.

But, there are sins and sins; sins of weakness and of malice, sins against God and against our neighbor, which, though all radically wrong, yet vary in intensity and degree. In hot inrushes of anger, or lust, some souls seem almost powerless against sin; whereas, in the case of many others, their cool, deliberate choice of evil makes their sins especially deadly. Such is the group of sins forbidden by the Second Commandment. There is a devilish malice about blasphemy and kindred offenses against God, that makes them particularly heinous. Even hardened sinners in other respects will instinctively put their fingers to their ears when blasphemers rail against God, or vilify His Holy Name. It seems a direct challenge of battle against the Most High. Hence we find that nearly all nations, howsoever low their religion, made this abuse of the name of the Supreme Being a penal offense, even when other forms of sin were tolerated or encouraged. By a perversion of this law, Socrates was doomed to die amongst the Greeks, and Christ amongst the Jews; the injustice of whose sentence is the greatest scandal in history. In the Jewish code it is enacted: "He that blasphemeth the name of the Lord, dying, let him die . . . whether he be a native or a stranger" (Levit. xxiv, 16).

Nowadays, it is high treason, and involves the severest penalty known to the law, to write, plot against, or defame men, "clad in a little brief authority." The humblest citizen in the land has a case in law against his maligner, but the "King of Kings" is defenseless, so to say, against the tongues of His creatures. The law protects the rights of men, but is silent or ineffectual about those of God. In olden days it was the reverse. Men then thought, as we "of the household" think to-day, that men's rights are best guaranteed where God's claims are respected. Now, putting these at their lowest, surely God must require that the great gift of speech— a free endowment of His to man—should not be turned against Him, and that the tongue should be used to praise and bless, rather than to profane and vilify His holy and adorable name.

I. As members of the Society of the Holy Name, we are here to protest against the abuse of one of God's greatest gifts to men; we are here to uphold respect and venerate the names that denote our Creator and all that refers to Him. No worse abuse and none more widespread than that of the Holy Name; and none, therefore, that calls more loudly for remedy. The evil is public and prevalent all the world over; and, therefore, private and individual efforts against it are of no avail. We must band together in groups and bodies. There are societies for every purpose under the sun. We have leagues against all crying evils—against gambling, against drinking, against impurity, against the evils forbidden by all the Commandments in short, and why not against those forbidden by the second? There is no society with a higher aim or loftier purpose, or more richly blessed and indulged by the Church. The Church herself is but a huge society for the promotion of religious life; in other words, for teaching the *use* and hindering the *abuse* of the holy and adorable name of God. It is her aim, and it is ours, that the name of God should be honored, loved and respected, not merely in church, but in street, field and factory. Were we all what we should be, and what we profess to be, there would be no need for societies of the Holy Name; but we have fallen on evil days, when men, who owe their very being to God, are ashamed to utter His adorable name in prayer or praise; and yet deem it manliness to profane it, in cursing, swearing or blaspheming.

Therefore, I say, we must club together in holy brotherhood, to make war on this gigantic evil. Union is strength. Water in drops is the weakest and most helpless of elements, but crowded into streams and rivers and oceans, it is the most powerful and resistless of all. Detached rays of light or heat effect nothing, but how remorseless they are when concentrated in a furnace, or pouring down in torrents from a burning sun in a cloudless sky. Each Society of the Holy Name must be as a river, to cleanse away on its march all foul, irreverent, blasphemous usage of God's name; and in the reverent use of it, ever send forth from their own hearts and lips, a stream of fervent prayer and praises to the Most High God.

II. The object of the Society of the Holy Name is, therefore, twofold, first, to engage in a crusade against the profanation of God's name under all forms of utterance whatsoever; and next, the advancement of the blessing, praise and honor due to it, both in ourselves and in others. We live in a period of social endeavor. We must work in groups. Individualism is played out. The idea advocated by the one universal Church, that humanity is one family, that *fell* together and must *rise* together, is coming to the front. Our efforts to spread the devotion and honor due to the Holy Name must not be limited to ourselves or select coteries, but must leaven the masses. We must scour the "highways and byways" of life, and force all men to come in. Anyone who duly honors the name of God is, to all intents and purposes, a member of the Society of the Holy Name.

But active membership implies more. It means active warfare against the abuse of God's name. Just glance at what this means. Climb each step of the social ladder, from the lowest to the highest, and we find varying abuse of God's holy name. Let us walk along the street, take our stand among the throngs of idlers there, follow men and women into mills or shops or factories, go out into the fields, where Nature, in all her changing moods, invites the reverent invocation of our Creator's name—and what do we hear? God's name—if not ignored or banished, employed only in profanity and ribaldry. Mount higher. Enter the schools and colleges, the universities and the lecture halls; mingle among men that work in the great departments of the state, enter into the courts of law, where justice is solemnly administered in the name of God, and the heart of the reverent is saddened by the widespread abuse of God's holy name—cursing, swearing, perjury—everywhere rampant. Nay, even in the pulpit, that professes to mold the religious thought of the day; to say nothing of the platform and the press, there is a great deal of irreverent use, if not of downright blasphemy, heard. Here is work for members of the Society of the Holy Name. It covers in its negative aspect, we may say, the whole ground of the second Commandment. "Thou shalt not take the name of the Lord thy God in vain"—the importance of which we may judge from the fact that it is the only one to the transgression of which a direct Divine threat is attached— "The Lord will not hold him guiltless that shall take the name of the Lord his God in vain" (Ex. xx, 7). If there be a language in hell, it must be surely one wherein cursing, perjury, oaths, in their worst and most hideous forms, profanity and blasphemy make social intercourse unbearable.

And, indeed, we may say the perjurer and the blasphemer give one, even in this life, a foretaste of the horrors of the under world Listen to the ribaldry, profanity, cursing and swearing that go on in some parts of the great human hives in cities. Watch all the great antichristian forces at work to-day in the state, in society, in the great schools of thought, and you will see them steeped in blasphemy, i. e., "working together with Satan for the ruin of souls" All these we have to oppose—nay, wage unrelenting war against them.

Furthermore, our object is not merely to suppress the *abuse* of the Holy Name, but to promote its *use*. Ours is not only a work of *destruction*, but of *construction*. Besides uprooting the kingdom of Satan, prince of blasphemers, we have to plant the kingdom and reign of Christ. Now, this means that, in addition to refraining from cursing and swearing, we must ever praise and bless His Holy Name. Some of God's worst enemies avoid cursing and swearing, and yet sin, and sin grievously, too, by never using the name of their Creator at all; who ignore Him, refuse to acknowledge Him—who never bend the knee or raise the heart or voice to the Being who made them. A godless life, such as theirs, is a wicked, an irreverent and a perilous life. Prayer and praise and blessings are strictly due by the creature to the "Lord of all might and power." To fail in this duty, i. e., not to invoke the Holy Name—not to acknowledge or appear to recognize God in His own house, the universe, is an *implied* insult, a silent indignity offered to His Name. The tongue that fails to bless God, the heart that banishes Him, is accursed. What we say of the individual we may say of the race or nation. The people that ignore God; that drive Him from their midst, that exclude Him from law and education and public life, can not be blessed. They can not be a happy people, whatever else they may be, for they are wicked or on the way to be. "For my people have done two evils. They have forsaken me, the fountain of living water, and have digged to themselves cisterns, broken cisterns that can hold no water" (Jer. ii, 13). "Thy own wickedness shall reprove thee, and thy apostacy shall rebuke thee" (Id. ii, 19).

III. Were men what they should be; were Catholics particularly, consistent with their professed belief—the love of God should burn in every heart and His praise ever rise from all lips. They would be steeped in God. Now, to bring this ideal state of things partly about, we must make the prayerful use of God's Holy Name a factor in our lives. We must breathe it. It must, as fragrant incense, be ever ascending from heart and voice. The highest function of a creature—as it should be his highest privilege—is prayer and praise, in other words, the *reverent use* of the Holy Name. This is the positive side of this Commandment. It is the main duty of the members of the Society of the Holy Name.

I have chosen the "Divine Praises," therefore, as affording subject-matter for a few discourses, to be addressed to you during the coming year. It was a blessed thought that prompted Pope Leo XIII to make their recital obligatory after the function that ranks next in the Church to Holy Mass. They are all ways of honoring the Holy Name and helping us to carry out the end for which our society was formed. Each will afford the heading of a conference, and, with God's blessing, help us to appreciate their depth and beauty. Their frequent utterance will be a safeguard against abuse of the

Holy Name, and a powerful means of building up the kingdom of God in our souls.

We are all, in our measure, called to bear witness to God in the world; to "bear testimony" to Christ, to "confess Him before men." Now, membership of the Society of the Holy Name is an open avowal of our belief in, and love of God and His Christ. And what more effectual means of discharging this duty than the devout recital of the Divine Praises? In every sovereign state, whether republic, empire or kingdom, the name of its ruler or recognized head, strikes both eye and ear at every turn—in press, in stamps, on coins and public buildings. So in the kingdom of God within us in our own souls, and in the Church at large without us, must the holy and adorable Name of our Supreme Ruler be ever witnessed to, and heard. Be it ours ever to love, honor and respect the Holy Name of God, under all its forms and bearings. Leagued together in holy and united brotherhood, let us go forth into life's highways and byways as living witnesses to the truth and influence of our holy religion. Let us never allow ourselves to be tempted in public or in private, in office, street or factory, to take part or show approval, of cursing, swearing, blasphemy, or any other profane or impious use of the Holy Name. Let us, on the contrary, ever bless, praise and adore it; and both by word and example, teach others to do the same. Thus, on our lips, at least, shall God's name be "hallowed," and the prophecy of Malachy fulfilled: "From the rising of the sun even to the going down, my name is great among the Gentiles" (Malachy i, 11).

II.   "BLESSED BE GOD"

"Benediction and glory, and wisdom, and thanksgiving, honor and power and strength to our God for ever and ever."—Apoc. vii, 12

"And I heard a voice from Heaven, as the noise of many waters . . . . and the voice, which I heard, was as the voice of harpers harping on their harps."—Apoc. xiv, 2.

*SYNOPSIS.—I.   The first of the divine praises finds an echo (a) in the world of matter, (b) in the world of spirits.   The words, "Blessed be God" are but a summary of the great hymn of creation to its Framer. Apparent discords strengthen harmony of universe.*

*II.   Promotion of good use and repressing of bad main object of Society of Holy Name.   World meaningless if its chief purpose of the glory of its Creator not achieved.   As body of man a synthesis of matter so his soul is of spirit.   Both combine as hymn of praise to name of God*

*III   (a) Efforts of Church to keep stream of prayer and praise in honor of God's name ever in movement.   Liturgy, divine office, well termed "Opus Dei"   (b) Counter stream of fetid blasphemy in opposition to this   An atmosphere of blasphemy encircles some places. (c) How thinkers depending on unaided reason debase the grand idea of God witnessed to in Catholicism.   Leads to abuse of His name.   False, crude views make false gods.   Idolatry a witness hereto. shows need of God and danger of error.   Same in new Paganism, Monism, Pantheism and the rest   Truth about and due reverence for His name enshrined in Catholic belief.   Outside theology run riot.   Bodies, not individuals, ever entrusted with revelation.   Jewish nation and church*

*IV.   The abuse of God's Holy Name in cursing.   What is implied in cursing   Lessons.   Duties.   Exhort to good use of God's Holy Name.*

I.   The first of the "divine praises," "Blessed be God," seems to be an echo of these beautiful words of St John, the natural outburst of a soul that contemplates God in His works.   Nature around and the starry heavens above, to any one at all impressed with the grandeur, order and rhythm reigning throughout, are as a great hymn of praise, voicing the attributes of God, singing out as "harpers harping on their harps," "Blessed be God," "Bless the Lord all ye his works."   What seems to the jaundiced eye of the pessimist, or the ignorant and the godless, a riotous world, "where there is no order and everlasting horror dwelleth," is to the learned and devout a great harmony where each jarring discord falls into its place around a great central theme—that can not be better expressed than by the words of the angels, "Glory be to God on high," or of holy David, "Oh, Lord, how admirable is thy name in all the earth," and echoed by us to-day when we repeat, "Blessed be God." If any work of art, *e. g.*, a great poem, a great painting, a great building, forms a song of praise to the author, how much more does that great work of art, the universe, the house of God, "made without hands," bear witness to Him, who framed, and even upholds, it in "the might of his power"? If we reflect at all we must feel that we are walking in a temple of awe and mystery, where God rules and reigns supreme. Overwhelming evidence of His presence, though silent and unseen, and yet everywhere around us. His power, His wisdom, His providence are felt in every cloud that flits across the sky, or blade of grass that bends beneath our feet. In storm and flood and earthquake, when our earth momentarily seems a rudderless ship, or one broken loose from control, we particularly feel how helpless we should be were the arm of "the Lord God our Governor" shortened or withdrawn. From the depth of our weakness and dependence we can but cry out, "Blessed be God," "Praise, honor and glory be to his name forever "

As in speechless worship the heavens thus "declare the glory of God"; so in rapturous and intelligent adoration does the heavenly host, the great spirit world, that fill up the space between our souls and God, join their voices in the same strain. The great hymn of creation is thus complete. If in some mysterious way creation does not voice this great, and alone intelligible, purpose, it would be a jarring and unmeaning puzzle indeed. Free will (for God would have free service) may appear to thwart and mar it in part, but it only secures it more perfectly as a whole. Discords are essential factors of harmony. They do but lead to a fuller, deeper and more sonorous expression of the divine praises: "Blessed be God" forever and ever.

II. It is to this great work of blessing and praising God, of making our frequent invocations of His Holy Name ring out as sweet melody in His ears, that we members of the Society of the Holy Name are specially called. No doubt war upon cursing and swearing and blasphemy is likewise incumbent on us; but the main purpose, the grand aim of our work is, while uprooting the *abuse,* to extend and foster the devout *use* of the Holy Name of God. To adore, praise and bless His Holy Name is the highest function, as it should be the chief pleasure and loftiest privilege of man. His bodily structure evolved from "the slime of the earth," is a marvel of divine workmanship, that is itself a hymn of praise, representing the lowly material elements from which it sprang. So should his soul, that came from God, and links man to the angels, be in its varied powers and activities a song of praise, voicing the mute inferior creatures he is deputed to rule. No other purpose can explain his mission in the world. The fall interrupted, but did not change, man's work of praising and glorifying God.

When we say that by reason man is raised far above the beast of the field, we do but express half a truth. It is not so much the *gift* of reason, as the *exercise* of it, in blessing, praising and adoring God, that raises man above the brute, and makes him "a little less than the angels." The man who never uses his reason in the service of God, who never utters the words "Blessed be God," who never prays, and, worse still, boasts of never praying, who, if he uses the name of God at all employs it only in cursing, swearing and blaspheming, is immeasurably removed from the beasts, not *above,* but *below* them.

III.   Hence the Church, main defender of God on earth, both in reason and faith, ever invites men to give full vent to their religious instincts, nay, to leave in spirit the very world that God made our home, and devote their lives mainly to praising and blessing His Holy Name.   Day and night, all the year round, the great stream of liturgical prayer streams forth from her choirs of angels in the flesh, called aside to serve the sanctuary, expressing incessantly the first of the divine praises "Blessed be God."

And not merely from her chosen bands of devout religious men and women; but from the hearts and tongues of thousands of her other children, mounts a grand joint act of reparation for the hideous and nameless outrages to which the adorable name of God is subjected.   For we are, alas! compelled to own that alongside the current of praise and blessing to the true God, there ever rises a fetid noisome atmosphere of profanity, swearing and blasphemy. Over many of our large cities a thick pall of smoke often hangs suspended, fitting image of the dense cloud of blasphemy against God that rises from them.   He is thereby shut out, debarred access to His creatures, so to say.   His nature is obscured and darkened. The light of His countenance no longer shines upon them.   Be it ours, therefore, to dispel, as far as in us lies, this darkness as to God "that covers the face of the abyss."

Never before, perhaps, did the true children of the Church need to cry out, with deeper faith and fervor, "Blessed be God."   For one of the worst signs of the times is the tendency to debase the grand idea of God, witnessed to by the Church, and the very pearl "of our Christian inheritance."   Thinkers of the day are tampering with the concept of a God, free, almighty, creator of heaven and earth, and presenting us with one, "made in their own image and likeness." For while men no longer fashion their gods in wood, clay or stone, yet none the less they give us false presentations of the one true God, and so dishonor Him. Turn away from the traditional idea of a pure, free Almighty Spirit witnessed to in the old dispensation, manifested in our Lord Jesus Christ, and upheld in our Creed, as the Father Almighty, creator of heaven and earth, together with all the light cast on this idea by the teaching Church, and you have a false god, a process that in religion surely leads to profanity and blasphemy against the true. The only perfect idea of God, whose existence and attributes it is our privilege to defend, is enshrined in Catholic belief. Revelation only and special guidance in preserving it can guard the measure of the true knowledge of God communicated to man both in reason and faith. The true Church is the only safe guardian of both in this respect. Outside her schools theology runs riot.

It is worthy of note that the treasure of the knowledge of one self-existing Supreme Being, who made all things, was entrusted to a family, a nation, a body, God's people, the Jews, and from them passed to their successors, the Catholic Church—the kingdom of God on earth. Individuals, it is true, using reason aright, may and do rise to the knowledge of God, but imperfectly and haltingly. As for the masses sunk in material needs, engrossed with material cares and pleasures, it is morally impossible for them to reach the knowledge of the true God. Light must come to them through authorized teachers. It is worthy of note that for this purpose not individuals but teaching bodies have ever been chosen. To the Jewish nation under the old dispensation and the Church in the new was the light of revelation entrusted and the mission imparted to spread the light and keep it burning. It is no doubt true that even outside these bodies God had witnesses; but they were official guardians of the truth and upheld it nationally. Belief in Him certainly is too plainly testified in the world and in man's mind and conscience to be ignored; but the human heart is so depraved that truth gets dimmed, tarnished and corrupted. Thus idolatry witnesses both to man's need of God and at the same time his proneness to debase the idea of God. Yet bad as idolaters were and are, yet in their reverence for their false gods, in their execration of those who swear falsely by their names or blasphemed, they mutely reproach those who deal so irreverently and profanely with the being, attributes and name of the one true living God.

Many, alas, to-day, "once enlightened," are falling into a worn form of idolatry—an idolatry of man—of self, of the world, without the excuses or self-sacrificing rites and duties of the old. Be assured, then, that outside the stream of Catholic thought and tradition the knowledge of the living God, "maker of heaven and earth," "the king of ages," free, personal, almighty, falls away into unreason and impiety. It is still true that "salvation is of the Jews" (John iv, 22), *i. e.*, truth in religion lies with those that God entrusted with its guardianship. We must still go up to Jerusalem —the new Jerusalem—to worship in spirit and in truth. God's prayer and praise must still be "in the church of the saints." We have still, as of old, to "praise the Lord in his holy places," as well as "in the firmament of his power." "For the Lord is well pleased with his people, and he will exalt the meek unto salvation" (Ps. cxlix, 4).

We may say, then, that our meek and lowly Society of the Holy Name has to do in each district what the Church does for the world at large, keep the torch of the knowledge of God alight, uphold the truth of His existence and attributes; and both by precept and example teach men how to honor, respect and reverence His Holy Name. It is a noble work surely, to defend our Creator's rights, in His own realm, to be convinced ourselves and to convince others that we live even in this stormy world under a canopy of love, and that the attitude of all toward Him should be expressed in the words "Blessed be God." "The praise of him is above heaven and earth." It is thus we must tune our harps, *i. e.,* our lives, ever to praise and bless God's Holy Name.

IV. Alas! that there should be so many exceptions to this rule and that so large a number of the free creatures of God should invoke His Holy Name not in blessing, but in cursing. "May the name of the Lord be blessed from henceforth now and forever" (Ps. cxii), are the words that should spring from the lips of all "who call upon the name of the Lord"; but cursing is the direct contrary of this. It is asking Almighty God, who "loves the work of his hands," who in the beginning pronounced everything He had made good, to use His might—turn His power against His own creatures, and inflict evil upon them. God in Scripture is said to open His hands and fill with plenty every living creature; but one who curses prays God to "rain down fire from heaven" upon them. "God is love," but cursing is not merely a sin against the law of love, it goes farther, and prays the God of love to aid and abet us in heaping evil on those we dislike. What greater perversion of the great gift of speech? What baser ingratitude to God, "who forgives us our trespasses seventy times seven," than to ask Him to sanction what is most opposed to His divine nature, hatred, anger, revenge. Cursing, *i. e.,* the invoking of evil on others, is the very antithesis of God's work, in creating, redeeming and saving His creatures. In His infinite wisdom He declared all things good that He had made. And when the masterpiece of His hands had used the highest endowment bestowed upon him by God to compass his own undoing, God came in person to seek and save His lost sheep—a work that He is still carrying on through the ministry of His Church. Now they who curse would dare to ask the Almighty to destroy, to punish, to undo, in short, His work of mercy and love. Men are here to bless, love and help each other, not to curse and wrong one another. No wonder cursing is called the language of hell, for it creates a hell where it is habitually practised. Cursing is the utterance of thoughts and desires most opposed to and removed from God. Where God is not in love there is hell. It recoils, too, in self, as we see in the case of the Jews in the wilderness and their descendants at the Crucifixion. "He loved cursing and it shall come unto him" (Ps. cviii, 18).

Thus to touch on cursing in a theme on blessing seems like striking a false note in music, but in reality the evil of the abuse of God's name in cursing sets off the beauty of its use in praise and blessing. Darkness enhances light. Discord and strife are the dark background that make us realize better the beauty of union and peace.

Be it ours, then, as members of the Society of the Holy Name, to wage relentless war on the habit of cursing, now so rampant in the world, though so hateful to God and baneful to man. Let us destroy any lingering tendency to this habit in our own souls, and thus we shall be better fitted to cope with the evil in others.

We can find no better means than reflection on what our religion tells us about Almighty God—who He is, and what He does for, and is to, us. It is inconceivable that anyone, seriously doing so, can dare to profane or dishonor His Holy Name. Let us, then, make reparation for the abuse of the Holy Name and ever repeat it in prayer, praise and blessing—frequently reciting the divine praises, and above all "Blessed be God."

### III. "BLESSED BE HIS HOLY NAME"

"From the rising of the sun unto the going down of the same, the name of the Lord is worthy of praise."—Ps. cxii, 3.

*SYNOPSIS.—A sea of mystery lies hid in the short word—God. Imbedded in every language and religion. Linked with the remotest past yet the most vitally living word in use. Is a living stream of wisdom, an inexhaustible mine of knowledge. Answers all questions of mind and heart.*
*I. Sadly debased in idolatry and impiety like pearls in slime or diamonds in coarse clay is the most precious word in world of speech. Bears witness to universal belief in supreme being. Souls thirst for God. Universe soaked in God. Is necessary truth—an axiom and a postulate of thought. Holy Name sufficient reason for all truth. Why ignored and disbelieved. Not a harmless theorem or problem, but ethical truth implying duties and consequences Adequate knowledge of God impossible, but known withal Pure and holy are never sceptics.*
*II. But Holy Name is more than a casket of sublime thoughts It reminds us we are creatures, Christians, members of a society the object of which is to promote the cult of the Holy Name· all of which involves special duties. What these duties are. Meaning and evils of sin of perjury. Exhort to avoidance of swearing and veneration of the Holy Name of God.*

*Introduction.*—The second in order of the divine praises forms the theme of our discourse to-day. A word or name is the embodiment of a thought; but there are single words in a language so suggestive, so full of meaning, so far-reaching in their application, as to be very seas of thought. Now of these words "that speak volumes" the Holy Name of God is the principal. Some old words, like fossils, bring back the past—a past replete with history, poetry and romance; but the word God, though one of the oldest in the language, is yet ever the freshest and most forcible, a living stream of wisdom—a fountain, a storehouse, a mine of inexhaustible knowledge; because it denotes the infinite Being, who ever was, is, and will be. The word is imbedded in every language, and lies at the root of every form of religion. It meets us at every turn in life, whether we peer into our own souls or out into nature. It is the answer that springs to the lips of all, sage or peasant, child or man, when we ask: "Who made all things? and where do they come from?" It is the wisest answer, too, because ever a true, and often the only one, we can make to inquiring minds. It fits all inquiries, whether the matter be a flower or a star, the boundless sea or the boundless universe. That the word "God" should be debased is no proof against its worth.

Pearls and diamonds are earth's most precious treasures, even though hid away in slimy oyster beds or rough clay and rock. True, the word "God" lies often buried in idolatrous rites; it is heard on the tongues of the perjurer and the blasphemer, it is lightly and profanely uttered by the heedless; yet it is the loftiest, the most pregnant, and the most sacred word in the world. Wheresoever and howsoever coined, it bears the stamp of the Creator, and is a living witness to His existence. In varying degrees of vividness and force it speaks out the belief of mankind as a whole in a first cause—a supreme uncreated being, whose existence is thus a necessary postulate of thought. The learned may choose to call it the *absolute,* the *unconditional,* the *infinite,* but all these resolve themselves into the simple term, God—who, if He does not inspire love, must at least inspire awe. If we don't bless His Holy Name, we must fear it. Indeed, both form the duty of the creature.

Hemmed in by His overwhelming might and majesty, what else can we poor mortals do but cast ourselves reverently at His feet exclaiming: "O Lord, how admirable is thy name in all the world" (Ps. viii, 1), or if crushed by a deep sense of guilt, cry out with penitent Thais: "O thou who hast created me, have mercy on me."

I. What a consoling thought withal! In reverent boldness we can draw near to God and, as children who prattle out the endear-

ing terms of father and mother, familiarly address Him as Father
Almighty. Both mind and heart thirst for God as the "hart pants
for the living streams"; and God fully sates their longings. One
condition only is required on the part of those who come to these
living fountains, the vessels must be clean. "Blessed are the clean
of heart, for they shall see God." The devout utterance of the
Holy Name, therefore, makes God as near and as visible to the
clean of heart, and the clean of mind, as the sun at midday. It is
only the blind and the befogged who would then presume to doubt
of the sun's presence. So with God in the world. The world is
steeped in Him, plunged in Him.

There is no existence so evident, no being so manifest as God
He is a necessity of thought. His existence is a truth, if not
axiomatic, at least of immediate inference; like self-existence,
or personal identity  All minds in whatsoever molds they are
cast, in looking for a cause or reason of what surrounds them, fly
at once through all intervening causes to the Holy Name of God
as sufficient reason, in ultimate analysis, for everything. Space,
and time, and science are all transcended both by mind and heart,
in search of God, wherein to rest. But we have not to travel far,
inasmuch as "he is not far from each one of us, for in him we live,
move and have our being." He is with us in His Holy Name.
Therefore thrice "blessed be his Holy Name." And yet there are
godless men—men on whom the "light of His countenance never
shines," in whose breasts His Holy Name awakens no echo, souls
to whom the world is an enigma, the heart a desert waste. There
are men who hate the name of God, who, if they could, would
banish it from the heart and blot it out of the language. There
are others who, without going so far, would tell us that we neither
know, nor can know if there is any personal being at all answering

to the name of God; and that if there is, He is both unknown and unknowable—a being quite outside the range of finite and limited faculties, such as ours.

There is but one answer to all these cavillings against the contents of the Holy Name. "Taste and see." Purify the heart and He will shine into the soul, like the orb of day. The truth involved in the Holy Name of God is not like that contained in a mathematical problem. It is more than a theorem. It is practical. To believe in God implies the relations of a creature to its creator, relations that impose *duties,* or, in other words, burdens, not always easy to flesh and blood. The root of atheism and its synonyms is in the heart. The holy and the pure-minded, whether wise or unlettered, never doubt about God—a much stronger argument than appears on the surface. To say that the infinite is beyond our capacity to comprehend, that the idea expressed by the term "God" is outside the reach of created intelligence, is either a truism or a quibble.

Undoubtedly God is incomprehensible. He would not be God if He were otherwise. The finite mind can not grasp the infinite. Were our faculties magnified a thousandfold, were our intelligence equal to that of the highest angels, it would still be incapable of realizing the full meaning of the Holy Name. The grounds for agnosticism exist in heaven as well as on earth, if it is based on the incomprehensibility of God.

Knowing God to the extent of our powers is a very different thing from knowing Him adequately, or not knowing Him at all. The tenderest flower that grows, the tiniest insect that flies, have something of infinite mystery about them that God alone knows. Withal who would say they are to us unknown and unknowable? No more is Almighty God. Though incomprehensibility is of His essence, though "his ways are not our ways nor his thoughts our thoughts," yet "the eyes of all look to him," to rest both heart and mind in His adorable name, as a term that explains all mystery and settles all the weary doubts and questions of the day. The adorable name of God is in itself a book of divine wisdom; but its treasures are oft "hid from the wise and prudent," and revealed to the little ones. Unless we become as little children in humility and truthfulness, we shall never master the philosophy of the Holy Name. The humble of mind draw wealth from its utterance, but the proud are "turned empty away."

II. But not merely does the Holy Name suggest sublime and beautiful thoughts, it reminds us of the relations we bear to the great Being to whom it is applied. It reminds us that He is Creator and we creatures, the work of His hands, and that as *responsible* beings we owe Him duty. We are bound to Him by ties, rooted in knowledge and love—we owe Him service. This loving service is specially binding on us, as members of the Society of the Holy Name who have pledged ourselves to defend it against abuse—to make reparation for outrages committed against it, and bring home to ourselves and others the treasures of wisdom, peace and comfort it contains. No wonder that the name used to convey the great concept of God to the human mind should be held as the most sacred in the language; and that there should be an express command given by God Himself to secure it due honor and respect. Even among men, one of the first duties we owe a neighbor is respect for his good name. A breach of it in certain cases may entail the highest penalty prescribed by law. Can we wonder, then, that "the Lord will not hold him guiltless, that shall take the name of the Lord his God in vain" (Ex. xx, 7).

One of the first duties of a creature besides the worship of his

Creator is to be jealous of the honor of His name, to love, honor, respect and vindicate it on every possible occasion. No more fitting expression of these feelings can be found than in the devout and oft-repeated utterance of the divine praises "Blessed be God," "Blessed he his Holy Name." Among those who thus hallow and bless the Holy Name there is no danger of its being ever "taken in vain," howsoever frequent its use. They will ever speak of God as they think of Him, *i. e.,* with love and reverence—ever confessing, and bearing witness to it—defending and upholding the great affirmation it contains—and as opportunity offers, reproving, instructing, and guiding the sinful, the poor, the young, the ignorant, in all that relates to the holy and adorable name of God; so that all may join us in ever saying from the heart "Blessed be God's Holy Name."

Devout souls, filled with that feeling of God's presence which the frequent use of His Holy Name must inspire, will never venture to criticize His works in a carping or pessimistic sense, will never murmur against the arrangements of His providence; and even in pain, grief or loss, howsoever deeply they may cut into the soul, will always "praise and bless the name of the Lord," who is Lord of life and death, free "to give and free to take away."

They who are thus steeped in the spirit of the "divine praises" will ever speak with becoming reverence, not only of the divine name, but of all holy persons and things that derive their sacred character from association with Him—such as the saints and angels, the Holy Mass and Sacraments, the sacred rites and ceremonies, the Church, her ministers, and her laws; for all are meant to bring us into closer contact with Him for whom the Holy Name stands. Indeed, any honest expression of religious conviction is to be respected. Religion in any form whatsoever, provided it is a *bona fide* effort of the soul to get into touch with God, and keep peace with Him, even though it be but a perversion or caricature of the only true religion, is good, immeasurably better than utter atheism or rank godlessness.

Many say that religion is dying out; but it can no more die than the mind or the heart of man can die. If we embrace not the true, we have to create a false one. It is a need of the soul—like idealism or romance. And on this instinct of human nature must we, the members of the Society of the Holy Name, work to bring men round to a knowledge of the true God and deep veneration of His holy and adorable Name.

But, above all, cult of the Holy Name brings with it respect for the sanctity of an oath. When we solemnly vow, promise or swear to anything, and call God to witness the truth of what we say, a special sanction is impressed on our act, that renders its violation perjury. Perjury is a sort of high treason against God—and an outrage on His Holy Name. How dreadful it is to reflect that any human being, aware of what is meant by the term God, should deliberately invoke Him, the infinite Truth, to stand witness to the truth of the lying statements that fall from his lips. To be false to one's fellow men, to pledge their credit or forge their name, to foreswear one's gambling debts even, is deemed mean and disgraceful; but to lie to God, to disregard the solemn vows and promises made to Him, lightly to take oaths, and call Him to witness what we know to be false, is deemed nowadays of little consequence; though a reprehensible abuse of the Holy Name of God. To say nothing of one's Baptismal promises, so often renewed and broken, of the vows made *in* and *out* of religious life, and so often left unfulfilled—what terrible perjury both accompanies and follows the

Sacrament of Marriage. The great institution that starts the streams of life—the very wellhead of the race, becomes a very fountain of perjury.

The abuse of the Holy Name by false swearing is one of the leading sins of the day. Perjury, that used to stand in the fore-front of crimes, is now looked upon in some quarters as a trivial offense, especially when bearing on the most important and sacred relations of life. I need not further say how painful it is for those who revere and bless the name of God to hear it so often invoked frivolously, rashly, unjustly, and unnecessarily. It is for us mem-bers of the Society of the Holy Name, who are leagued in a sacred crusade against the abuse of the Holy Name, to let people know, both by word and example, that it is no light or trivial matter to call upon the great God, whose "name is terrible in all the earth," to stand as witness to a lie, or add piquancy to profane and ir-reverent speech. Let us resolve ever to refrain personally from this vice, and by mutual endeavor and loyal co-operation strive to root it out of the circles in which we move. It is a gigantic evil, and must be met by earnest and united efforts. To strengthen us in this contest we must dwell reverently on the thoughts suggested by the Holy Name of God, invoke it in prayer, respect it when we hear it uttered, and frequently repeat the divine praises "Blessed be God," "Blessed be his Holy Name."

IV. "BLESSED BE JESUS CHRIST, TRUE GOD AND TRUE MAN"

"Praise ye the Lord and call upon his name. . . . For great is he that is in the midst of the holy one of Israel"—Isaias xii. 4-6.

*SYNOPSIS—Defense of Holy Name of Jesus main object of Society of Holy Name Its charter in fact Same law that forbids abuse of name of God forbids also that of Holy Name of Jesus Source of contention because Jesus, "Set for fall and resurrection of many." Burning question of day, "What think ye of Christ?" We fearlessly frame our answer on that of St. Peter and expressed in divine praises as "Blessed be Jesus," etc. Our Lord dishonored by being put on level with other founders of religion. His divinity not a matter of texts or even reasonings—of faith, resting on living voice of Christ Himself in church How words of Isaias, Christ's own statements and actual belief of Church confirm His divinity. Denial hereof leads to denial of God. Fraud*

*II. We live in a critical age. Nothing in matter of belief escapes almost hostile scrutiny. Religion, too, brought under miscroscope. Weighed in balance, yet not found wanting. · Our Lord dogmatic, self-assertive; Church the same. Upholds her great affirmative in spite of criticism—even in her devotion. Belief in divinity of her Founder goes to very roots of religion. Is gift of God in faith? What it implies. Special duty of members of Society of Holy Name to defend Our Lord's Godhead and repel blasphemous criticesms. A man stands at summit of spiritual plane. His grandeur springs from His divine personality.*

*III. Blasphemy against divinity of Christ springs from dividing living Christ from living Church. How and why? All own to His lofty human character, but forget or ignore that it is rooted in His divine personality.*

*Conclusion.—Exhort to study of Christ's claims as God and man War against unbelief. Source of blasphemy. Exhort to knowledge and imitation of Christ.*

*Introduction.*—As members of the Society of the Holy Name we have undertaken not only to defend, vindicate, and honor the name, rights, and claims of Almighty God, the Supreme Being; but also those of Emmanuel, "God with us," in the person of Our Lord and Saviour Jesus Christ. With the same feeling of deep love, homage and veneration that we exclaim "Blessed be God," are we likewise to utter, "Blessed be Jesus Christ, true God and true man"! The same divine law that forbids us to take the name of God in

vain likewise forbids us to dishonor the Holy Name of Jesus. Indeed the rescript establishing the erection of the Brotherhood of
the Holy Name had specially in view the "most sacred name of
Jesus," for the prevention of cursing, swearing and blaspheming.

It is sad to reflect that the name of Him who was "meek and
humble of heart," whom even His enemies, when challenged, dared
not accuse of sin, whose name is a synonym of all that is "high,
holy, and of good repute," should be a bone of contention, an
object of blessing and cursing, of divine honor and ribald blasphemy; in other words, that He should be "set for the fall and
resurrection of many in Israel." This comes necessarily from
the stupendous question still put before men, and forcing an answer,
that determines whether we shall grant or deny divine honor to
"Jesus of Nazareth, King of the Jews," "What think ye of Christ?
Whose Son is He?" Clinging to Him, "who has the words of
eternal life," and mustering round our spokesman Peter, whose
rock-built faith will never perish, we hesitate not, amidst the jarring theologies of the day, to exclaim, "Thou art Christ, the Son
of the living God"; and we are here to-day to reaffirm this confession, in a prayer, that if Christ were not God it would be a
blasphemy to utter, "Blessed be Jesus Christ, true God and true
man."

Our veneration for the Holy Name of Jesus does not spring
from our interpretation of a few isolated and hotly disputed texts,
nor is it the halting conclusion of a halting line of argument; but
rests on the inspired and living voice of a Church teaching a
divinely inspired creed. Far from thinking that we honor Christ,
as some think they do, reckoning Him with Socrates, or Buddha,
or Confucius, or other founders of religions, we deem such association sheer blasphemy against the name of God and a gross breach

of the Second Commandment. Even they who speak and write so unctuously of the *"divine"* in Jesus, and describe Him as the "highest manifestation of God in creatures," are far from giving condign honor to the name of the Being, "in whom dwelt the fulness of the Godhead visibly," who "had the words of eternal life"; and who, centuries before His appearance in the flesh, was portrayed by the prophet to the people as "God the mighty," "God with us," "Father of the world to come" (Is ix, 6), and as "God himself come to save them" (Ibid. xxxv, 4). We take His own words for the truth of the terms in which we address Him, for they are "spirit and life"—words that are declared in Scripture to be still living and effective, "These words which I have put in thy mouth shall not depart out of the mouth of thy seed's seed henceforth, now and forever." It is this divine teacher of the race, still living and speaking in His seed, spiritually speaking, that we listen to, in the Creed. The Catholic Church is His generation, *i. e.*, an act of His creation, and ever breathes His spirit, and utters His words. Though it may prove a "stumbling block to the Jew and a folly to the Gentile," yet, ever true to her mission, she refuses to consider any claims or titles adequate to express her belief in the nature and personality of her Lord, save those voiced in the prayer, "Blessed be Jesus Christ, true God and true man."

We make no distinction, therefore, between this profanation of God's name and of Christ's name; for Christ and God are in the divine nature, one and inseparable. "Philip, he who seeth me seeth the Father," and, consequently, we may add, blasphemy against Christ is blasphemy against God. In both cases the Holy Name is profaned, and a violation of the Second Commandment incurred. To speak injuriously against Christ, His person, His attributes, is to take the name of God in vain. To be Christ-like is to be Godlike. Hence, to be one with Him, to mold our character on Him, to put Him on, to live Him, is to live God—it is leading a divine life. We invariably find that those so-called Christians who begin by tampering with the divine nature, personality, and attributes of Christ—who would cast out Christ-God from their minds and hearts—who would replace the divine Christ by a merely human one, drift, by a sort of fatalism, into utter irreligion and godlessness. We have an object lesson in France. Herein we find the oldest Catholic state in the world practically proclaiming itself atheist. Taken as a body, men's deepest and most persistent instinct is religion—a need of the soul that, in some form or other, has ever found expression in their public life. A godless people is unknown to history. Yet here is a people doing all they can to remove even the name of God from every department of state—from their very buildings even. His name no longer appears in their coinage, as if it were a sort of treason to ask His protection for their country. Now this apostasy from God began with apostasy from Christ. Nowhere has the attack on Our Lord's divinity been more virulent and blasphemous than in their land. In their press, and literature generally, scorn, ridicule, and blasphemy, all weapons that hatred could devise, have been employed to crush Christ and His ideals. As always happens in the case of those "once enlightened" when they fall away, "abyss calls upon abyss." Turning from Christ leads steadily down to the pit of utter godlessness and irreligion. Christ and God are one. The Church, whose mission is to witness to both, invites us to join in an act of solemn reparation and worship in the words, "Blessed be Jesus Christ, true God and true man."

II. The present is an age of revolt against authority. There is a veritable craze for negation and doubt. Primitive truths, facts of history, all grounds of belief are either denied or scrutinized in a critical or doubtful spirit. We can not wonder, then, that religious truths should not pass unchallenged. But with this difference: The claims of religion, in doctrine and practise, rouse either the deepest antipathy, or most devoted enthusiasm. The Church, as we see, reproduces the life of Christ, who ever stirred up the rage of His enemies, or the devotion of His friends. To the denials, and taunts, and threats of His foes, He ever opposed a calm, unimpassioned statement of His claims. "Amen I say to you," "He that is not with me is against me, and he that soweth not with me scattereth," "Before Abraham was I am." No proof is given, no reason offered, any more than when light pours in on reason or conscience. He claims to bind both the mind by truth, and the will and heart by love, or law, and that, too, by appealing to the authority given by "him who sent me." To their curses, their mockeries, their jeers, and their blasphemies He opposed only silence, or the reaffirmation of His claims. He does the same in and through His Church to-day. To the outpouring of her enemies by tongue and pen, to their ribaldry, abuse, and slander, she reaffirms her undying faith in God and Jesus Christ. She prays aloud that they may be blessed, praised and glorified. To those who would exclude doctrine from prayer, and make all religion a mere matter of feeling or sentiment, she answers by making dogma the very basis of devotion, "Blessed be Jesus Christ, true God and true man." We must know Our Lord before we can love Him. Instruction in doctrine must precede devotion. The will, the seat of true devotion, must not be the sport of mere sentiment or emotion. It must be guided by an enlightened mind. Even duty itself is grounded on dogma.

For belief in Christ's divinity goes down to the very roots of religion in the soul. The whole fabric of our holy religion is based on it.  All our practises of piety are involved.  Christ, whom we adore as God, is the sun and center of our faith.  It is the conviction of the reality of His Godhead, as well as of His manhood, that fills us with reverence for His name and makes the profane use of it a sin.  How this great affirmation should come to be accepted and defended even to the effusion of blood, by the most learned and devout of all races, amidst the crumbling beliefs around, can only be fully explained, as was its first confession by St. Peter, in Christ's own words, "Flesh and blood hath not revealed it to thee, but my Father who is in heaven."  True, there are aids to belief—prophecy, miracles, Our Lord's own words; but to conclude that "God so loved the world as to give up his only begotten Son" requires a special light, a special grace—the grace of faith.

This grace is part of our inheritance as born into Christ's kingdom, the Church.  There we can "taste and feel how sweet the Lord is."  There we can ask "to put our finger, like Thomas, into his sacred wounds," have our eyes opened, as the apostles in Thabor, and see Our Lord transfigured, the sun and center of the goodly company of the old and new dispensations, of Moses and Elias, bearing witness unto Him.  We can thus see the King in His kingdom, fully carrying out His promise to be with His Church all days, and make her the mouthpiece of His spirit.  "We worship that which we know."  We have Christ God among us, and therefore can we say, "Blessed be Jesus Christ, true God and true man."

More than ever it behooves His true followers to rally round Him in defense of His person and His Church.  As members of the Brotherhood of the Holy Name we are, so to say, His bodyguard.

Profanation of His name, denial of His divinity, abuse of His

Church are direct attacks on Him; and against these it is our duty to wage undying war. The fortunes of a king are wrapped up in his kingdom. Christ is one with His Church. The outcome of revolt from her as His real, visible, tangible kingdom, wherein He dwells, body, soul and divinity, true God and true man, is to isolate Him, thrust Him back into history, as a dead hero, the founder, framer or creator of a system of morals or philosophy, and nothing more. It leaves a beautiful touching figure of the past, who uttered beautiful thoughts, and who, like so many idealists, came into conflict, and went down before the material forces of His day. Catchwords are used to replace the living Christ by one that is "neither true God nor true man." That He left us "the legacy of his sayings," "his example"; that He was "the highest type of ethical life," "a manifestation of the divine," are all mere phrases that show, not the *presence* of Christ, but the *absence* of God. It is tantamount to saying that the Christ, whom the most advanced and cultivated nations of the past nineteen centuries have worshiped as God, is only a creature, and that we blaspheme, rather than adore, when we utter the third of the divine praises, "Blessed be Jesus Christ, true God and true man."

III. All this blasphemy and unbelief comes from divorcing Christ from His spouse, the Church. He is as truly present now to the eyes of faith as He was in Bethlehem or Nazareth. The words of my text are still true, "Great is he that is in the midst of thee the holy one of Israel." Old-fashioned deists used to say that God "dwelt far away in light inaccessible," and left the world He had made to take care of itself. The current unbelief to-day is that He is so merged in the world as to be indistinguishable from it. The attempts of our non-Catholic friends to explain the reality of Christ's presence in the Eucharist usually end in con-

vincing people of His real *absence*. So with Christ's promise to
be with His Church till the end of time. If she is no more than "a
house of Rimmon," if Christ, as God and man, is not with her,
except in a mere figurative sense, if He is not now "reigning in
the house of David his Father," in His "kingdom without end,"
that kingdom, that house "set upon a hill to which all nations should
flow"; then he is dead and gone, or lives only in memory, as the
Son of Joseph and Mary. Howsoever beautiful His character, or
great His work, He would still be infinitely removed from "Christ
the Son of the living God," owned to by St. Peter and upheld by
the Church in all ages.

He is man, it is true, but it were blasphemy to say He is no
more. The loftiness of His human character springs from the
divine personality that swayed it. Other members of the human
family have reached great heights; but in the long roll of history
He towers far above all others. Indeed He is the center of history.
The most advanced and cultured nations reckon their dates from
His birth. He is admittedly the sun and center of the highest
form of religion that ever appeared in the world. Even pronounced
evolutionists in the sphere of morals and religion, tracing the
gradual ascent of man through the various stages of sentient, intelligent, moral and spiritual life, place Christ at the summit of the
spiritual and supernatural plane. Thus, whether holding orthodox
or unorthodox views of the personality of Our Lord, all own, with
St. Paul, that "Other foundation can no man lay but that which is
laid, which is Christ Jesus" (I Cor. iii, 2).

*Conclusion.*—We have laid special emphasis on Our Lord's
divinity. Nobody nowadays calls His sacred humanity in question
or denies Him a high place in history. He that founded the world-
wide Church and proclaimed the eight beatitudes as an ideal in

life must be great. It is His Godhead they ignore and deny. As members of the Society of the Holy Name we have a special work and function in His kingdom—to guard the honor of His name. The Holy Name is injured, is profaned, is blasphemed if men deny that Jesus is true God. Not heresy, but unbelief, is the great source of sins against the Third Commandment in our day. In the press, in fiction, in street and mart and school "ravenous wolves in sheep's clothing" spread the poison of infidelity. It is for us to learn the grounds of our belief, and, "strong in faith," to resist false teachers. Ours must not be a dead, but a living, faith. It is only they who model their lives in Jesus Christ, who live and breathe His spirit, that can fruitfully battle against His enemies. Let us ever beg Him to fill us with faith and love, and help us to spread knowledge of and devotion to His Holy Name. In heart and voice let us ever unite in saying, "Blessed be Jesus Christ, true God and true man."

### V.  "BLESSED BE THE NAME OF JESUS"

"Thou shall call his name Jesus, for he shall save his people from their sins "—Matt i, 21.

*SYNOPSIS.—I.  Associations that cluster around the Holy Name of Jesus. A name that has brought joys and blessings to all.  Is food, drink, and medicine to devout souls.  Its bearer, Brother and Saviour, King, Priest and Prophet.  A mysterious sweetness imparted to it  "Virtue ever goes forth from it," like radium, clay and rose.  Sad to reflect that a name of such sweetness should be abused.  How?  Duties of members of Society of Holy Name.  Many try to empty it of its full meaning. The word stands for same Being as that represented by dread Jehovah. Its very letters singly suggestive of helping thoughts  They tell us what He does for us*

*II.  Justifies by His grace  Transforms us into new beings—a new creation.*

*Enlightens us in all dark problems of life  How?*
*Saves us from our sins and their consequences.*
*Unites us to God—makes us one with Himself.*
*Sets our thoughts lastly on His being our Saviour*
*III  The very letters of the Holy Name tell us in condensed form what He, who is mighty, has done to our souls.  The monogram of the joint word Christ reminds us what Jesus expects from us.*
*Come to Him, for light, and leading, and healing.*
*Hear His voice in heart and conscience.*
*Receive Him when He asks admittance to our hearts*
*Imitate His virtues.*
*Serve Him with heart and hand, in time and eternity.*
*Trust in Him in all your needs.*

*Introduction.*—Next to the adorable name of God none holds higher rank in the world of speech than the Holy Name of Jesus. All that is comforting, all that is lofty, beautiful and holy, in thought or in language, cluster round the Holy Name.  It is light, food and medicine to the soul, says St. Bernard.  It is a word of love, a name, too, implying victory and power; and one that inspires such deep respect that "In the name of Jesus every knee should bow of those that are in heaven, on earth and under the earth" (Phil. ii, 10).  There is not a single human being, whether aware of it or not, who has not personally benefitted by Him whom this name denotes. For, to the world at large, and each member of the race singly, the bearer of it is a loving Brother, a Redeemer and a Saviour. To all and each He stands in the relation of king, priest and prophet. Language could not exhaust the tender associations with which the Holy Name of Jesus is coupled. To realize this we have but to cast a glance on the touching and beautiful epithets woven into the Litany of the Holy Name.

The test question of the hour in the religious world to-day, as among the Jews in Our Lord's time, still is, "What think ye of Christ?" In other words, what is the precise meaning summed up in the Holy Name of Jesus. As explained in a previous discourse, we give expression to our views of Christ when in the divine praises; we say, "Blessed be Jesus Christ, true God and true Man," words that do but re-echo the great confession of St. Peter, "Thou art Christ, the Son of the living God," thus anchoring our souls on the rock of faith. And if you ask why God appeared in the garb of man, you will find it in the words of my text, "Thou shall call his name Jesus, for he shall save his people from their sins."

Though there is a weird and unexplained savor about the Holy Name of Jesus, it is not the word itself, it is the bearer, who has breathed the soul of sweetness into it. Others bore the same name before Him—Joshua or "Jesus son of Nave, successor of Moses, great according to his name" (Ecclus. xlvi, 1); Jesus son of Sirach, and another Jesus son of Josedu, high priest in the days of the prophet Aggaeus (i, 1); but lo! it was bestowed on the son of an humble Nazarene; and it became, and has ever since remained, transformed into a name of light and love and healing, like the bread cast down from heaven, "having in it every kind of sweet taste," a name, too, of spiritual strength and victory, since,

"in the name of Jesus," men and nations, sunk in the lowest depths
of moral degeneration, cripples in soul, "rise up and walk," "in the
brightness of his rising."

Why? Because a word of human origin touched the vesture of
the most high God, and "virtue went forth from it." It has become the *radium* of the house of God. Light and heat stream from
it unintermittingly. "I dwelt with the rose, said the lowly clay in
the eastern fable, and that is why I smell so sweet."

How sad to reflect that a name, so inherently sweet and spiritual,
so powerful withal that angels bow and demons tremble at its
sound, should yet be daily and hourly profaned, and otherwise
abused! Men shrink from hearing a beautiful melody, that seems
to vibrate only to the purer and holier movements of the heart, set
to words that are low and debasing. It sounds like sacrilege to the
ears of those in whom there is any soul or sense of the beautiful
left. Yet there is no taint of sin in all this. It is only a matter of
good taste and feeling. How dreadful, then, must it be to hear the
Holy Name of Jesus sinfully used in cursing and swearing, in ribaldry and blasphemy. It is melancholy enough that a Name so
inherently sacred should be profaned and reviled by those who
either know not or believe not in the divine reality behind it; but the
abuse of the Holy Name in "the house of his friends," of those who
love Him, has a malignity all its own. And this is what rives the
heart, in some Catholic lands, when the ear is shocked by abuse
of the name of Jesus. Do they know, or can they believe in Him,
whose Sacred Name issues so blasphemously from their lips? Can
free will show greater excesses in divine mercy, greater forebear-
ance than in the permission of this unbridled abuse of the Holy
Name of Jesus?

As members of the Society of the Holy Name, therefore, be it our aim, as it is our work in the Church of God, to respect, and get others to respect, the Sacred Name of Our Lord and Saviour Jesus Christ. Let us, for example, resolve to bow the head on hearing it pronounced, a practise enjoined by the Council of Lyons, in 1274, and richly indulgenced by Sixtus V. Above all, we must frequently invoke it in times of temptation, danger and sorrow. As experience proves, it has magical, nay, almost sacramental power. There are men to-day calling themselves Christians who would fain empty the name of the Master of its true significance and substitute hollow, empty phrases for the real Jesus, "true God and true Man." It is ours to run counter to all this and convince men of good will that Jesus is "the Eternal Light," "the brightness of the Father," "the Eternal Word, who in the beginning was with God and is God." Though the name Jesus is one that inspires tenderness and love, yet it stands for the same Being of beings expressed in the Old Law, the law of fear, by the term Jehovah, a name of awe and majesty, that the high priest was allowed to pronounce but once in the space of a year. Now that we live under the law of grace and love, when all, "through Jesus, have access to the Father," let us frequently invoke God under His tenderest name—the Holy Name of Jesus. It should be engraven on mind and heart in letters of gold. Its every letter is pregnant with light and love. It is said "there are sermons in stones," so are there in letters—the letters that make up the Holy Name of Jesus. It is a sacred monogram, each letter of which will give us a thought. I have seen it stated that the letters of the word Jesus point out what Our Lord has done for us; while those of the word Christ suggest what we, in return, should do for Him.

J.   Jesus *justifies* us by His gift of sanctifying grace: through Him in the Sacraments of Penance and Baptism, or their equiva-

lents, we, dead in sin, are born again into the life of grace or holiness, *i. e.,* we are lifted up to the spiritual or supernatural plane of
life. We emerge as truly from the grave of sin as He did from the
tomb on the first glad Easter morn. Between us, dead in sin and
alive through His grace, there is the same difference as between a
lifeless statue and a living man, or as between a painted lily and one
that lives and blooms in a scented garden. Through the grace He
earned for us by His life, Passion and death, He bestows on us a
greater gift than life, a higher dignity than royalty. The power
whereby He justifies us is greater than that of fabled magic wand
or philosopher's stone. It changes the coarse clay of our common
human nature into the divinely refined gold that will glitter in the
streets of the heavenly Jerusalem. Nay, He makes us share in His
own divine life, a statement we should never dare to utter had
we not His own words for it, "I am the vine, you are the branches."
Grace is the sap that makes the branch one with the stem. Limitless
power impelled by limitless love can produce startling effects, both
in nature and grace. The one illuminates the other. Grace we see
not, but we observe its counterpart in nature, the plant transmuting
the coarse elements of the atmosphere and the soil into the leaf, and
flower, and fruit, in ever recurring life; and we thank and praise
God that Jesus the heavenly gardener is doing similar wonders in
our souls. Who will not, then, exclaim in accents of love and
gratitude, "Blessed be His Holy Name."

E. The second letter of the Holy Name tells us that Jesus, the
world's true light, *enlightens* "them that sit in darkness and in the
shadow of death." In the dark ocean of life He is posted as a light-
house "to give light and save life." "Behold I am with you all days"
to light up life's dark ways. The sun is His emblem. It is His
creation, illumining the world of sense. But He is likewise the

"sun of the soul," the true light of intellect—of all knowledge.
But there are problems too deep for sense and reason—problems,
too, of vast practical consequence, on which our happiness depends.
Herein too is He our soul's true light. He is in His Church to be
"a light to our feet," in the dark paths of faith and morals. His
spirit puts into her mouth the necessary measure of truth, and wards
off the power of darkness, from the teaching and guidance; so
that error may not prevail against her. He is with us in the Sacrament of the altar, to be in still more subtle and mystic way a
light to the individual soul. He is the light of the heart, as well as
of the mind. The very utterance of His Holy Name sheds light
upon the soul as sunrise brings the dawn.

S. The mid-letter of the Holy Name suggests our Lord's main
title of *Saviour.* "Thou shalt call his name Jesus, for he shall save
his people from their sins." Redemption—salvation, full, free, un-
trammeled, is His gift. "With him is plentiful redemption," "He
will redeem Israel from all her iniquities." The forty centuries that
preceded His coming represented a long drawn out sigh, mute often,
and unconscious, of our fallen race, for a Saviour to come.

Now that He has come and "stands in our midst, a sigh of relief
ascends from all hearts, inasmuch as we have seen the salvation of
Israel;" and have among us one to whom we can cry out in
danger and sorrow, "Lord, save us, we perish." Blessed, then, be
the name of Jesus, Our Saviour, "Who gave himself a redemption
for all," "Who washed us from our sins," by "Blotting out the
handwriting of death that was against us" (Col. ii, 14).

U. Again Jesus *unites* us to God, the center and good of our
being. All feel the need of this union. The very dream of thinkers,
the aim of all systems of philosophy is to reduce all to unity, to
make all one, creator and creature. It is only a dream; and yet

it shows the instinctive longing in desire of man for God. Indeed, all religion is but a striving to bring God and man together—a union effected in and through Jesus. In Him, the finite and the infinite, God and man meet. It was brought about in the Incarnation, in the only possible way in which it could be brought about and is being daily renewed among us. The wanderer from God, the prodigal son, the lost groat, is being sought for, to be brought back again to God. "In the lavor of baptism and penance for the remission of sins." Just souls are daily united still more strongly in Holy Communion. In a word He begins through grace the union that is to terminate in glory. He is the Alpha and Omega, the beginning and end and perfection of union with God in nature, grace and glory.

S. The letter "S" terminates the Holy Name, as if to rivet our attention, for the second time, on the thought that Jesus is our *Saviour*. New truths, moral and otherwise, need new words to express them. So the deep inward meaning, the new relation between God and man expressed by the word Saviour, *Salvator,* was undreamt of, till Our Lord came and "saved his people from their sins" Salvator was not good Latin, says St. Augustine; but Christ, in coming, made it such. Let realities in truth come; and words will not be wanting to express them. Jesus is ever *saving*—ever recovering lost souls, ever seeking starved sheep, lighting the candle and sweeping the house, in search of the lost groat, making all things new, and bringing them back into peace and harmony with God. Saviour is a word, indeed, that can be felt and relished, better than expressed. The thoughts it raises urge us to cry out with fervor "Blessed be the name of Jesus."

The Holy Name of Jesus is thus a condensed meditation on the great things that "He who is powerful" does to our souls. Its very letters remind us that He justifies, enlightens, saves, unites us to God by grace and adoption; and in every relation to life is our Saviour and friend. Worthily does St. Paul say, "There is now no condemnation in them that are in Christ Jesus." Who, it may be asked, are in Jesus? He tells us Himself, when likening Himself to the good shepherd, who gives his life for his sheep, He adds, "My sheep hear my voice." If the letters of the Holy Name Jesus tell us all He does for us, those of Christ seem to point out what we are to do to Him.

C. "Come to me," He seems to say, "and I will bestow on thee the wealth of wisdom that lies stored in the Holy Name of God, and of Jesus, true God and man." "This is eternal life that they may know thee the true God, and Jesus Christ whom thou hast sent." Put my name as a seal upon thy heart and lips, utter it only in praise and prayer in the spirit wherein Holy Church invites us to exclaim, "Blessed be the name of Jesus."

H. Hear His voice, when He speaks to you in conscience, in the voices of your superiors, and in the clear calls and inspirations of His holy Spirit.

R. Receive Him in your hearts, when He knocks for admittance. Cast Him not away, for it is only to "such as receive him that he hath given power to become the sons of God."

I. Imitate Him. He hath left us an example, that as He hath done, so also should we. We must build ourselves into His likeness. Salvation depends in our resemblance to Him. This is another way of saying "Take up your cross and follow me." It is, too, the secret of the king, that lies hid in the words "Learn of me, because I am meek and humble of heart, and you shall find rest to your souls" (Matt. ix, 29).

S. Serve Him. You call Him Master and Lord, and "say well,

for so he is;" but we must show the fruits of service in heart and hand, *i. e.,* in *love* and *works*. *Filial,* not *servile* fear must characterize our service. Holy fear leading to love is vigor and force in devout souls, who truly and deeply, not lightly and flippantly, honor the Holy Name.

T. Trust Him. He is a friend, indeed the only friend who never changes, and in whom we may ever confidently rely in good and evil repute, for time and throughout eternity.

VI. "BLESSED BE HIS MOST SACRED HEART"

"Where thy treasure is *there* also is thy heart."

*SYNOPSIS—I. The Sacred Heart tunes our hearts into harmony with God  Man alone among the beings that people this planet stands aloof from his Creator. Though alone capable of knowing and loving God, he is the only one that wilfully refuses to blend heart and voice in creation's hymn  Every human heart should be an organ of divine praise. In Christ we have one heart in perfect accord, able to pour forth free, adequate, all-perfect acts of prayer and praise. Religions an effort on man's part to render due worship; but imperfect till coming of Sacred Heart  Human and divine meet in Sacred Heart. Realizes the dream and sates the thirst of man for God  Union, but not commingling of God and creatures. Sole possible synthesis of God and man that so many vainly endeavor to es-tablish. Sacred Heart resolves all difficulties, unites all contraries, satis-fies all our cravings.*
*II. Sacred Heart not only atones for man's sins, but voices his prayer and praise to God  Divine worship first duty of creature  The psalter of David  Main theme, dominant note, praise. Christ central figure—the harpist; His Sacred Heart the instrument. What is praise? Recognition by creature of God's stupendous worth and merit.  We as finite call in aid of Sacred Heart in work of praise  Man ever drawn to God, but seeks Him wrongly  Sacred Heart teaches way. It costs, but answers to every need and tendency of the soul. The heart of the crea-ture before its Creator either faints away in awe, or pines away with love  Sacred Heart the divine mediator between them.  Love, zeal and self-surrender in cause of Sacred Heart specially incumbent on members of Society of Holy Name. Resolve, therefore, to show this: (a) In intelli-gence, by thinking of it; (b) in will, by loving it; (c) in act, by self-sacrifice; (d) in voice, by praising it.*

I.  To weary pilgrims, in the wilderness of sin and sorrow, called the world, the thought of the Sacred Heart comes as a re-freshing breeze.  Where Jesus is really present, there is the Sacred Heart, whether He shows Himself in a cloud, or pillar of fire, or manna from heaven.  In all cases He seems to tune our jarring and discordant souls into harmony with God.

We all own that man's heart and voice should freely and gladly re-echo the hymn of praise creation sings to its Maker: "The heavens declare the glory of God," but alas! the notes that should swell highest and clearest are often either silent or heard only in discords. The lord of creation, who, in mind and heart, holds the key to its mysteries, who alone is privileged to know, love and rationally worship his Creator, is the only one who profanes and blasphemes His Holy Name.

It is some consolation, however, to think that amongst so many hearts, prone to evil from their birth, given over to low, sordid, selfish, godless aims, quite foreign to the purpose for which they were framed, there is one great human heart free from all this, one heart sinless and unselfish, whose every impulse is an act of infinite love, atonement and praise combined  For, though a heart in form and tissue and function like our own, yet it is the heart of God incarnate; and its every beat of love, of hope, of pity, of worship is as truly divine and infinite as is the creation of a world.  A body was fitted for the Eternal Word, and in that body a heart was set, human, it is true, yet moved and controlled by a Divine Personality. The burning heart of Jesus is the symbol and synonym of Divine love.

Every human heart, in relation to God, should be an organ of love and praise; but too often, as I said, is it the seat and source of cold indifference, and hideous blasphemy.  Even at its best it falls infinitely short of capacity duly and worthily to praise and worship God.  Happily, we have in the Sacred Heart of Jesus, our brother, wherewith to glorify God, to plead, to love, to offer homage, to be represented.  This Sacred Heart lives our human life to-day in heaven, in the tabernacle, in our own breasts.  It does our very work for us, members of the Society of the Holy Name.  It atones for outrages and blasphemies against the name of God.  It observes on our behalf the Second Commandment in all its fulness.

Throughout all creation there is a mute, speechless adoration of the Being, who is its first cause. This reverence, adoration, and respect find, or rather ought to find, full expression in man's heart and voice. It has ever done so crudely, and imperfectly, at least, in religion, some element of which was ever visible, for to be religious, *i. e.*, reverent, in the face of nature, is to be human. But religion in all its forms, even the divinely sanctioned worship of the Jews, fell away into strange beliefs and practises, till restored by the Sacred Heart, who taught us the higher and better way, "made all things new" and reconciled us through Himself to God. This Heart answers the cry and thirst of the human heart for God, and whilst steering clear of the rocks and quicksands of pantheism, still brings God down to the level of his creatures. We have Him even more than *immanent,* we have Him incarnate, amongst us. Keeping the human and divine ever distinct and apart, we can worship the sinless and spotless heart of Jesus as Divine; and yet claim to use it, as human, in order to pray for us, and with us, as representing the heart and voice of humanity at large. In this manner, the synthesis of God and His creatures is realized in the ever blessed heart of the Son of Mary.

Certain forms of wisdom, old and new, blend God and His works into one confused whole. The world is ever evolving, making and unmaking itself. According to them, the finite and the infinite, the absolute and the conditioned, what we call the Creator and the creature, are blended into one great "all." As God can not be done without, the word is retained but divested of every trace of divine reality. Call it by what name they may, monism or pantheism, it is really atheism in disguise—atheism masquerading as religion.

It shows a need of the heart for the infinite—the craving of human nature to be united to the divine.

Now in the Sacred Heart of Jesus, as I said, we have this union

effected in the only possible way in which God and man can be
blended into one. Instead of the all pure, all holy God immersing
His adorable perfections in matter, or foul, loathsome, wicked souls,
He expresses Himself perfectly in Jesus Christ, "true God and
true man," whose Sacred Heart, main seat of life, becomes the
meeting point of the human and the divine. It is only in and
through Him that we can be united with God. It is at His sacred
fountains we slake our thirst for the divine. He is the vine, we
the branches; He the head, we the limbs of His mystic body, the
Church. But this union costs. The road to God by incorporation
with Christ, is narrow, steep and thorny. Many, all I may say,
seek God on easy terms. Hence few find Him, because unwilling
to pay the price. Christ is our mediator. He turns the rude, vile
metal of our good works into the gold coin "of the Kingdom."
He makes the praise, honor and glory we render to God of infinite worth. Such is the love of His Sacred Heart, that there
is danger in its making us too bold, daring, presumptuous, almost.
There is a risk in familiarity with the divine. Yet what would
life be without the Sacred Heart, without Him "into whose
hands the Father hath given all things" (John xiii, 3)? We look
up into boundless space and vainly try to count the worlds that
float in it, we look round at the mighty forces of nature and
measure ourselves, tiny atoms of matter and mind, with the Great
God, who holds all in the hollow of His hands; and the thought
strikes us speechless with awe, but, lo! we gladly call to mind that
"the Heavens have bowed down and sent forth a Saviour"; we
find Emmanuel, "God with us," in the person of the Man God,
pointing to His Sacred Heart, and saying, "Fear not, it is I.
Bless, praise, and adore my heart, give full vent to all your pent
up religious instincts before it; for though human, it is yet the

heart of God, it is human, yet Divine." It is strong, yet weak and tender and loving as a woman's. It is not a mere emblem of love; but loves, and lives, and vibrates in union with your own, in heaven, in the tabernacle, in your own breasts, when you choose to receive your spouse, in Holy Communion. Therein you find shelter from the world, consolation in sorrow. Love it, and you are loving God—praise and bless it, and you are praising and blessing the most High—worship and venerate it—give full vent to all the natural instincts of worship of a creature to the creator—make the words expressing it the soul's magnet, and you are but obeying God's voice, speaking in the first and second Commandments of His holy law. Who, then, will not fervently join in heart and mind and voice in repeating with Holy Church, "Blessed be His Sacred Heart"?

II. And this brings me to the main purpose of our reflections on the Sacred Heart, namely, that it furnishes us with an adequate organ of expression of the glory and praise we owe, one and all, to Almighty God. Not merely is it an instrument of atonement for sin, and especially for the worst forms of sin, blasphemy, and the abuse of God's Holy Name; but in addition blesses, praises, and worships God fully for us. It gives us support, and lends worth and value to our own poor efforts to discharge the great debt of praise we owe to Almighty God. His heart and lips voice ours. How intimately the word praise is interwoven with the word prayer, as a general term for our duty of worshiping God, we see in perusing that great volume of heart-offering, the Psalms of David. The Psalms are an ocean of prayer, ever fresh and odorous, though hoary with age. Now the psalter may be summed up in one expression: Divine praise, the antithesis of the abuse of the Holy Name, that it is our mission to uproot. What is

praise? Praise is the approval of merit, the honor we render to
excellence or worth. It is specially used to indicate the glad
tribute of homage and gratitude that we render to our Creator.
It is the great act of extolling, in ever varying ways, the great
God, "Who made heaven and earth." It is the glad outburst of a
heart, unselfishly "rejoicing in God its Saviour." How *shall* we,
or, rather, how *can* we, express the debt of praise we owe to Almighty God? In the Sacred Heart alone do we find an organ
fit to render worthy and adequate praise to God. One creature
only besides the sacred Humanity, the sinless and spotless mother
of the "Word made flesh," could truthfully say, "My soul doth
magnify the Lord," but we poor earthbound and soulstained sinners, what can we do but make use of the "child that was born to
us, the Son who was given to us," the "Emmanuel from on high,"
to praise, bless and adore God for us? In the daily sacrifice His
Sacred Heart renders full worthy homage to the Father for us
sinners.

What shall we worship and how, is the cry of the heart to-day
amongst souls no longer anchored to faith, and yet "athirst for the
living God." Alas! they are daily forsaking the Sacred Heart,
"The fountain of living water, and digging to themselves cisterns,
broken cisterns that can hold no water" (Jer. ii, 13). "Nations
may change their gods, for they are not gods; but my people have
changed their glory into an idol" (Ibid. v, 11).

Let us worship the world, say some, and all in it. We know
nothing else. Let us worship humanity, and its heroes, say others.
Let us join together, not in the service of God, but in the service
of man. Let us worship nothing at all, say most, but bask, like
the butterfly, in life's short hour. Folly! We can not escape
from God and the duty of praising and blessing His Holy Name.

The waves that break upon the shore, the light that gleams from countless suns, the birds that warble in the grove, the thunder that rolls in the sky, the cry of our own conscience within, speak of God, the duty of repentance and the obligation of ever habitually praising, blessing and adoring His Holy Name. There is a trumpet call heard from within and without us, "to invoke the name of the Lord," not in levity or profanity, not in cursing or swearing; but in ever recurring prayer and praise. But such is our nature that we want a being tangibly and visibly present amongst us, on whom to lavish these gifts of heart and mind. Like God's people of old, we must have our God in our midst, in tent, or cloud, or pillar of fire. Now, in the Sacred Heart we have more. We have not merely a sign or symbol, we have God Himself. His tents are spread not merely in the desert, but all the world over. A burning light points to His real presence in the flesh. He feeds us with the bread of truth, and the new manna, His own body and blood, so that "No nation has its gods so near to it as ours is to us."

In blessing and praising the Sacred Heart of Jesus, we are blessing and praising God. Through His adorable heart we enlarge the capacity of our own, and thereby elicit acts of divine praise and worship worthy of and commensurate with their object. In blending our offering of praise and prayer with the merits of the Sacred Heart, we merge our poor gifts in His infinity. In these evil days, when men will either not seek for religion outside of self, or turn the totality of creation into an idol they term God, and thus feed their souls, hungry for truth, on the husks of materialism, pantheism or monism, we have assuredly reason to be thankful for our knowledge of the Sacred Heart.

It is a consolation to feel that we can find in this Divine Heart of Jesus, an answer to every need and tendency of the soul—that in it we have God with us visibly—that His human heart beats in union with ours—grieving with us and rejoicing with us, ever teaching us what to say in prayer, and blending His homage and prayer and praise with ours. It thus stamps them with the die of infinite value, and enables us, through Him, to have easy "access to the Father." The iron and clay and brass we offer are transmuted in the furnace of His Sacred Heart into the purest gold that enables us to purchase eternal life.

The heart of the creature is moved by two feelings in presence of the Creator: One is to annihilate itself in humble adoration, "To faint away in awe and dread"; and the other is a longing to love Him infinitely, were it possible. Herein we feel the need of calling in the Sacred Heart to make up for our shortcomings, and offer, in our behalf, adequate love and worship. We feel all the more confidence, inasmuch as Jesus is one of ourselves—a brother in the flesh, that His Sacred Heart, though Divine, was yet the heart of a man—a real, true heart of flesh and blood, the adoration of which does not take away from the adoration of God in spirit and in truth, but rather brings God down to us, and makes us worthy to converse with Him in prayer, and pour forth our souls in becoming homage and praise.

But our devotion to the Sacred Heart must go beyond mere homage and praise. It must extend into the sphere of action. Head and heart and hand, knowledge and love and works, must go together. Thoughts and words are buds and leaves; but acts of self-sacrifice are fruits of true devotion. We gauge the love and zeal one professes by the degree of self-sacrifice or self-surrender he is willing to undergo for his beloved.

What then do we do and what are we prepared to do to show our love of the Sacred Heart? As members of the Society of the

Holy Name, special marks of love and reverence are required. We are missionaries. It is our work and a work of love to guard, defend and honor the Holy Name, and surely the Sacred Heart is a name for Jesus. It stands for the most vital organ of Jesus— an organ, too, that is a symbol of love. Now, God is love. The devotion that brings us into closest touch with divine love brings us nearest to God. In no heart is the Holy Name more revered than in one to which the Sacred Heart is dear. The divinest thing in being is pure, unselfish love. It is the highest form of worship. Faith and hope are also acts of homage, but they are only the foreground of love. It is the product of the heart. It is the key of life—the force that moves the world. Just think of the torrents of love that have gushed forth from human hearts since a human heart first began to beat; and yet mingled and united together, they would fail in the sight of God to equal in force and intensity a single act of love of the divine heart of Jesus. Together they are still human and finite, His is divine and infinite. Yet that Heart ever beats for us, pleads for us, makes atonement ever to the outraged majesty of God for the awful abuse by intelligent crea- tures of His Holy and Adorable Name. What we need to-day in religion is love and the self-surrender and self-immolation that go with love. Our model herein is the Sacred Heart. Hence the Church calls on us to bless, praise and worship the Sacred Heart. She herself is its organ. She holds our Lady's place on earth. She is a moral person with mind and heart. In her mind are mirrored the great truths taught by Christ and expressed in her creeds and dogmas. In her heart love shows itself in her devotions—the latest and most popular being devotion to the Sacred Heart. We, too, are the mouthpieces of the Holy Ghost in doing the work of the Church. She bands us together. She approves our rules—enriches their observance with indulgences.

Let us, therefore, in conclusion, resolve to study the wonders of divine wisdom underlying devotion to the Sacred Heart. Knowledge begets love and stimulates to action. Let us display this knowledge by true devotion—*i. e.,* a ready will to carry out the mind and will of the Master in our regard—*i. e.,* holiness of life. "This is the will of God, your sanctification." Lastly, for it is our special call and duty, to join by word of mouth in praising, blessing and defending the Sacred Heart and its claim on men's love and gratitude—ever ready to say with the voice of the Church, "Blessed be His most Sacred Heart."

VII. "BLESSED BE JESUS IN THE MOST HOLY SACRAMENT OF THE ALTAR."

"I am the living bread which came down from heaven; if any man eat of this bread he shall live forever."—John vi, 4.

*SYNOPSIS.—What the above expression, sixth in order amongst the divine praises, implies. Texts illustrating this Eucharist is but another name for Jesus truly present on our altars Hence duty of members of Society of Holy Name to rally in its defense.*
*I. Men hungry for truth and reality Lies and shams odious, especially in matters bearing on belief and conduct. If we ask for bread we do not want to be offered a stone; or a fish and be handed a scorpion. We trust to Church who holds teaching of Christ. Clearly put in gospels; promise in sixth chapter of St John; institution in these synoptic gospels. Faith a condition of belief. Furnishes evidence wanting to sense God can do all not involving contradiction, terms and development of doctrine*
*II. Power of God, acting through ministry of priests in virtue of supernatural law, determines presence of Christ on altar Not a creative act, or descent from heaven or bringing from other places, but simply change—a conversion of substance of bread. Nature has its laws, so also order of grace. Nature furnishes bread and wine; grace body of Christ.*
*III. May be viewed as Sacrament and Sacrifice Effects of words of consecration Sacrament permanent, not transitory Holy Communion fills man's natural thirst for God. Vastness of God's love herein.*
*Eucharistic rite also sacrificial Holy Communion personal Holy Mass public and social Is soul and center of religion How?*
*Duty of members of Society of Holy Name in relation to Holy Mass and Holy Communion.*

The holy Eucharist received in the form of Holy Communion, or offered to God in Holy Mass, "for the living and the dead," all the world over, is the sun and center of divine worship. More honor, glory, praise and thanksgiving mount to God on high from it than from all other sources of worship combined. And no wonder, for it is Jesus Christ Himself, "true God and true man," in the most holy Sacrament of the altar, "taking flesh, and offering Himself to His Father." It is the mystery of Bethlehem and Calvary; it is the Incarnation and Word and death, and uniting Himself not to humanity in general, but to each individual in particular. "It is Jesus of Nazareth passing by on the way of human life," whose very shadow can heal the blind, and lame, and devil-tormented of our race. "I am the living bread come down from heaven . . . he that eateth my flesh and drinketh my blood *dwelleth* in me and I in him" (John vi, 51-57). "As often as you shall eat this bread and drink this chalice you shall show the death of the Lord till he comes" (I Cor. xi, 26). "The ministers of God and the dispensers of the mysteries of Christ" (Ibid. iv, 1), *i. e.,* the new Christian priesthood, have replaced the doomed Jewish altar by "the table of the Lord"; so that "we have an altar, whereof they have no power to eat who serve the tabernacle" (Heb. xiii, 10). Thus we realize in our midst to-day, "through the blessed Sacrament," the new altar, priesthood and sacrifices, foretold by the prophet Malachy (i, 10, 11). "For, from the rising of the sun to the setting thereof my name is great amongst the Gentiles, and in every place there is sacrifice, and there is offered to my name a clean oblation, for my name is great amongst the Gentiles, saith the Lord God of hosts. In that day there shall be an altar of the Lord in the midst of the land of Egypt."

It is most fitting that we, the members of the Society of the Holy Name, should unite in defense of this great central mystery of faith. The word *Eucharist* is a divine name, for it is "Jesus in the blessed Sacrament of the altar." We rally round the banner of the Holy Name in upholding the reality of the divine presence in the tabernacle; and in doing our best to stem the tide of blasphemy and profanity uttered against Jesus in the Sacrament of His love. Let us enter devoutly into the full meaning of what is involved in the sixth in order of the divine praises—the subject-matter of our discourse to-day.

I.   In questions of science and history, and, much more, in those
bearing on religion, men hunger for truth and reality.   Empty
phrases, void of meaning, are but husks and chaff to a soul "athirst
for the truth of the living God."   What to believe, and what to do
in order to be saved, are matters of supreme importance surely to
all and each; and yet nowhere is it so true to say, that when men
"ask for bread they are handed a stone, or seek for a fish and are
given a scorpion" (Luke xi, 11), as in questions of right belief
and right action.   Happily for us, the words that convey the
great truths taught in the Scriptures and traditions about God
and our Saviour are not mere hollow sounds, denoting the inner
persuasion and conviction of certain men or nations; but real
truths for our guidance in life.   Such truths as the Trinity, the
Incarnation, the Resurrection, are not subjective opinions, but objective realities.   In no instance is this more applicable than to the
present subject.   In the great Eucharistic mystery with which we
now deal, God hath left, as the prophet foretold, "A memorial of
his wondrous gifts, he hath given bread to them that fear him,"
*i. e.,* "himself the living bread," that was ground in the Passion—
the grapes that were pressed and trampled into the wine—of His
blood, and which He enjoined us to *do* in Holy Mass, in remembrance of Him.   The extravagance of love involved in Christ's
real presence in the blessed Sacrament, like the folly of the Cross,
and the Incarnation, is a rock of scandal to many who, like
those disciples who first heard of it from His own lips, "refused
to walk with him," *i. e.,* ceased to believe in Him.   And yet it is
a truth that Christ's own words and acts have placed in Scripture beyond all reasonable doubt.   No unprejudiced thinker can
read the sixth chapter of the Gospel of St. John, wherein this
startling doctrine is most broached and premised as well as the ac-

count of its institution given by the three synoptic evangelists and
St. Paul, without coming to the conclusion that "the holy Eucharist is the Sacrament which contains the body and blood, soul
and divinity, of Our Lord Jesus Christ under the appearance of
bread and wine."

No doubt it is a "hard saying," and like all other mysteries and
miracles, appeals to that spiritual insight, called faith, as a condition
of belief.  As in the parallel case of the divinity of Christ, flesh and
blood hath not revealed it, but the "Father who is in heaven.
They "who judge according to the flesh" cannot enter into "the
spirit and life" of the words that bring in "this bread from heaven."
The light to see Jesus really present in the blessed Sacrament,
must come from above: "Therefore did I say to you, that no man
can come to me unless it be given him by my Father" (John vi,
65).  The lamp of the sanctuary symbolizes the light of faith by
which "the Father draws all to himself and Christ"—and helps
us to see God, either hidden behind the veil of nature—the veil
of our humanity, or under the elements of bread and wine.  We
leave to others the responsibility of impugning the plain words
used by Him "who has the words of eternal life" in both the
promise and institution of this mystery.  They were never modified
nor explained till the world was startled by a denial of them in
this obvious sense; and the Church was led to employ terms that
put the mind of the Master on the point beyond cavil and doubt.
They are summed up by the council of Trent, decreeing that Christ
is *"really, truly* and *substantially* present in the Eucharist," words
that have crystallized into the one expression, *transubstantiation,*
which indicates the change or conversion of the substance of bread
into that of the body and blood of Christ.  God's Church is the
world's teacher in matters of divine faith, and can, therefore,

choose and explain her own terms. She used words not verbally found in Scripture to express Our Lord's divinity, at Nice, and our lady's maternity, at Ephesus; and so, too, in the present case

If you ask how anyone, in flat opposition to the evidence of his senses, can bow down and worship the body and blood, soul and divinity of Our Lord, under the mask of bread and wine, I can only say that faith supplies defect of sight and furnishes evidence transcending that of the senses, "Praestet fides supplementum sensuum defectui." The sense of seeing, aided by telescope or microscope, discerns a new world hidden from the naked eye; so does faith in the sphere of the supernatural. Even if there were no illumination of the mind the conviction it inspires would enable the mind to assent with unerring certainty. What is not intrinsically impossible God may do; and we have His word for it, that He does effect this change. To prove it *impossible* we should know adequately the inner nature and essence of the terms body and substance, as well as the extent of God's power—a degree of knowledge utterly beyond us. All we can say is that anyone who reads dispassionately and devoutly the parts of the gospels and of St. Paul's epistles bearing on the matter, will be reasonably satisfied that this wonderful change, resulting in the real presence of Our Lord in the blessed Sacrament, does actually take place. This conviction deepens as we follow the history of the doctrine, and the branching devotions ever accompanying its development that mark this history from the Gospel age till our own. How this change is effected, like the other unsolved mysteries of nature and grace, we must leave to the power and will of Almighty God.

II. We reverently bow our minds in submissive faith to the belief that when the words of consecration are uttered in holy Mass the substance of the bread and wine is changed into the body and blood of Christ by the power of God, acting through the ministry of His priests. There is no creative act either on the part of God or man. It is blasphemy to say that in the Mass "the priest makes his god and eats him." We show God's gift in the Eucharistic food, as in all others. Our Lord's sacramental presence does not imply His descent from heaven, nor His being brought to the altar from any place, nor the annihilation of the bread, nor a fresh creation of Our Lord's body; it implies only a change or conversion of substance. Our Lord's glorified body, somewhat like a spirit, is not subject to laws of space and time. He is not in the host "circumscriptively," as is said, *i. e.*, subject to its dimensions. He is there sacramentally. He has chosen the *species* and sensible appearances. They both mark and mask His presence. When they are moved, He is moved. When they are reverenced or treated disrespectfully so is He. Sacrilege, as St. Paul tells us, lies in our not distinguishing or discerning the body of the Lord, "He who eateth and drinketh unworthily eateth and drinketh judgment to himself, not discovering the body of the Lord" (I Cor. xi, 29).

We say of nature that it is the vesture of God; we say the same of the sacramental species. They condition and mark His wonderful sacramental presence. The accidents of bread remain as a reality when their substance has gone; for the Sacrament must have them as an external sign. Their existence, no doubt, is a miracle. The Eucharist has a philosophy, a history, a poetry all its own; and yet as a truth of faith it is logical and consistent, and bears the closest mental scrutiny. It is as clear and logical in expression as any other revealed truth. For the supernatural has its order, its laws, its sequence of cause and effect, as well as the natural. Nowhere do the two orders blend and cross more than in "the blessed Sacrament of the altar."

Nature furnishes the bread and wine, symbols of love, from the union of so many grains of wheat, and the presence of so many grapes; whilst grace contributes the richest and rarest gifts in God's treasury. Nothing less than the body and blood, soul and divinity of His Son. Thus, elements that in nature most stimulate bodily growth are made, in grace, the main vehicle of spiritual growth. Unlike other Sacraments, the matter and form disappear, but the Sacrament remains in the emblems of the bread and wine. Like Christ Himself, it had its types and figures in the old law, such as the tree of life, the pascal lamb, the manna, the loaves of proposition, the food of Elias in the desert, the various sacrifices of the old law; and in Our Lord's own day, the change of water into wine at Cana, and the miraculous increase of the loaves and fishes.

III. The blessed Sacrament may be viewed in a double light, inasmuch as it is both sacramental and sacrificial. As a Sacrament it has the usual three essentials, the outward sign, in the bread and wine; the inward grace, in its communication of the very author of grace, Christ Himself; and lastly, divine appointment as clearly stated in the narrative of the last supper; and in Our Lord's previous promises to grant men this gift.

Once the magic words of consecration are pronounced, the same effect, by a law of the supernatural order, takes place as when they were first uttered by Christ, at the last supper. The body of the Lord lies on our own altars. It is no visionary or subjective presence created by the faith of the onlookers or the communicants; but the real objective reality, that on bended knees, we adore in the host. This real presence persists as long as the outward ele-

ments remain in their integrity. The ancient dove-shaped tabernacles in which it was reserved for the sick and dying, and the
custom of carrying it away for the use of anchorites and others,
attest the belief of the Church in Our Lord's abiding presence in
the "blessed Sacrament of the altar." The ever-growing pomp and
splendor of the ritual accompanying its cult, and the many devotions to which it has given rise, bear the same testimony. Daily
Communion, i e , incorporation with Jesus Christ—the nearest approach to living a divine life—the full realization of man's craving
for God and of God's for man, was the rule of the early Church,
as a return to it is the express wish of the head of the Church
to-day. Great as is the capacity of the human heart for love, broad
and deep as are man's views of God's power, he could never have
conceived such a stretch of infinite might and love, as are involved
in the Eucharist. Surely the Church, the guardian of the Eucharist,
may say, "There is no other nation so great that hath Gods so nigh
them, as our God is present to all our petitions" (Deut. iv, 7).

The vastness and complexity of the material universe crush and
awe us into a profound sense of our weakness and littleness; but
the immensity of God's love, shown in the Incarnation; and its
continuance, the Eucharist, lift us up to a sense of our spiritual
grandeur, and the lofty estate from which we fell. The Eucharist
is God seeking His own again—bringing back, by the very violence
of love, His erring children. Our souls are from God, our bodies
from nature; and in Holy Communion God unites Himself to us
in both. It is the absorption of the human back again into the
divine, whence it sprang. The change that Holy Communion
works even in world-tried souls, the straining toward God—the
ever-flowing stream of prayer and praise and silent worship, issu-

ing from the lips and hearts of myriads all the world over, at all hours of day and night—quickened and braced and tuned by the silent and lonely occupant of our tabernacles, clearly show all this. More than others does it behoove us who may be called knights defenders of the Holy Mass, to glorify, honor and revere Christ. God and Lord, under His Eucharistic name and titles; and be ever ready to cry out, with deep faith and love, in answer to the blasphemies pronounced against the Real Presence: "Blessed be Jesus in the most holy Sacrament of the altar."

But the Eucharistic rite is not merely sacramental; it is also sacrificial. Not merely is it Holy Communion, the great Sacrament of personal union and sanctification, it is the Holy Mass, the great solemn sacrifices publicly offered to God by men as a body, to carry out the four great duties we owe to God of adoration, thanksgiving, satisfaction and petition. It is the sun and center of our religion. All our main doctrines and devotions revolve round it. From the last supper onward it ever has been, and will be the central rite of Catholic worship. The Church at her Lord's bidding will never cease to "do this in remembrance of him," and thus "represent his death till he come."

It has been ever deemed an essential part of religion to testify to the supreme dominion of one's god by a sacrificial rite. Man's needs, and God's rights, required it. Merely internal sacrifice was deemed insufficient. The highest and most cultured, as well as the lowest and most degraded, nations offered sacrifices. Sacrifice, therefore, is not an outgrowth of savage fear or terror, but the religious instinct, inherent in rational nature, taking the form of some outward offering—whether holocaust, thank offering, peace offering or sin offering.

The Mass was prefigured in the sacrifices of the old law. It replaced them, inasmuch as it was their completion and fulfilment. The earliest Christian writers ever speak of it as verifying the clean oblation, which, according to the prophet Malachy (i, 11) should be offered "from the rising of the sun even to the going down of the same."

Where the Church of Christ is, there Mass is said. It is her very life and soul. It is her *"liturgy,"* her work on earth—her *raison d'être;* for in and through the Holy Mass is God worshiped and man sanctified.

No wonder that the power of hell is ever centered on the abolition of the great Eucharistic sacrifice of the Mass. All persecutions aim at this. Hatred of Church is mainly seen in efforts to corrupt, degrade, banish or slay her priesthood, and thus hinder the daily sacrifice and reception of Holy Communion.

It is for us, lovers of Christ's Church, defenders of His Holy Name, to prove our appreciation of this great gift of God, the Eucharist; to approach it frequently in Holy Communion, and assist at its celebration, reverently and devoutly, in Holy Mass. Thus shall we verify how sweet the Lord is and feel drawn to repeat frequently and fervently, "Blessed be Jesus in the most holy Sacrament of the altar."

VIII.    "BLESSED BE THE GREAT MOTHER OF GOD, MARY MOST HOLY"

"Behold from henceforth all generations shall call me blessed."—Luke i, 48.

*SYNOPSIS—Introduction.—Alive is angel's greeting and Elizabeth's salu-
tation. Depth of meaning involved in the two expressions, "Son of God,"
"Mother of God." "They found the child with Mary his mother" (Matt.
ii, 11). Mother and Son—Jesus and Mary ever inseparable in type and
reality.*
    *I.    Highest and noblest work of God next to sacred humanity of her
Son   Defense of her name and prerogatives part of duty and work of
Society of Holy Name; is strongest outpost of religion.   Dragon ever
pursues her.   Clear historical connection between growth of dogma concerning person of Our Lord and cult of our Lady.   One counterpart of
other.   Sermon on Mount and Magnificat.   Present doctrine and devotion
logical sequence of annunciation and decree of Ephesus   What world
and soul and body of man tell us of God.   Man great even as a ruin
The ideal; reality ever falls short of it   Ideas in God's mind true reality.
Our Lord and Lady ideal types of manhood and womanhood of race.*
    *II.    Glance at words of seventh divine praise.   Besides title of Mother
of God our Lady was blessed, great and holy.    (a) How and why
blessed?   In office, in grace.   Does not hereby obscure Christ.   Illumines
Him as dawn does day, as work its artist.    (b) How and why great?
Greatness depends on the share one has of God's gifts.   Well balanced in
her character.   Was "strong woman" of Scripture.   Great in intelligence;
hence seat of wisdom   Great in strength of will.   How and when displayed.    (c) How and why holy?   Holiness at summit of God's gifts.
Brings us nearest to Him.   Saints stand aloft like snowclad mountains,
Mary their queen and model*
    *Conclusion.—Exhort to zeal and chivalry in defense of name and
privileges of the "Great Mother of God, Mary most holy."*

In the seventh of the divine praises we repeat the thought expressed in the angel's greeting, and St. Elizabeth's salutation of our
blessed Lady.  Words are said to be coin to the wise, and counters
to fools.  Be this as it may, terms of tremendous import are in daily
use without our ever adverting to this profound significance.  We
barely heed, much less grasp or sift out what they mean.  Take
the two expressions "Son of God" and "Mother of God."  Except in a shadowy, haphazard sort of way, have we ever realized

that God was born a babe, that He was carried about in a mother's arms, that He drew life and strength from the living fountains of a woman's breasts, that under her loving care He "grew up in wisdom and grace before God and men"? "And entering into the house they found the child with Mary, his mother, and falling down they adored him" (Matt. ii, 11). The words are just as applicable to the house of God to-day as to the humble cave of Bethlehem. The mother and child are inseparable. The high altar and the lady altar are never far apart in God's house. The woman of Genesis is the maiden of Nazareth. Her seed is the babe of Bethlehem. She is the new ark of alliance, the dawn of the world's true light, the Sun of justice. She furnished the materials out of which His humanity was woven. She is God's masterpiece and "magnifies" Him who framed her.

I. We have dwelt upon the divine praises bearing on the humanity of Jesus Christ both in the Incarnation and its continuous presence amongst us in the blessed Sacrament of the altar; and we now come to speak of the created being, next in dignity to her Son Jesus Christ—her, I mean, graced at Ephesus with the title of "Deipara," mother of God: "Blessed be the great mother of God, Mary most holy."

It is our duty and mission, as members of the confraternity of the Holy Name, to war against abuse of God's name. So likewise is it our duty to respect the name and guard the honor of His mother and most richly endowed creature, Mary. In feeling ourselves bound to bless and praise, and protect against profaning the Holy Name of Jesus Christ, by parity of reason, it is a call of duty to act likewise toward the name and prerogatives of His holy mother. In doing so we are contributing to the fulfilment of her own inspired prophecy and command, "Behold from henceforth all generations shall call me blessed" (Luke i, 48).

More than half the profanity and blasphemy that shocks the godly springs from ignorance or habit. Could any human being dare to blaspheme God wilfully, knowing and reflecting on who God is? The same is true of our Lady. Men speak slightingly, or not at all, of her, because they know her not. The language of Catholic piety seems to them strained or exaggerated, because they know not the exalted place she deservedly holds in Catholic thought Though no goddess in our belief, she is yet her Creator's master-piece, one in whom the divine perfections shine more resplendently than in any other created being, save the humanity of her Son Jesus Christ. If we offer any form of cult or worship to a crea-ture, it is not for what they are, or have of themselves; but because they reflect the beauty and perfections of God, just as a painter, a poet or sculptor is almost deified in his work. We worship the divinity in the created humanity of Jesus, why not the divine ele-ment in Mary, whence Christ's humanity, body and soul, sprang. When we claim more than ordinary honor for Mary, and band together in defense of her name and privileges, we are in reality defending the citadel of the Christian faith in its strongest out-post. We have seen, and indeed are witnesses, to-day of how belief in God, and the worship and praise of God's Holy Name die out, or tend to die out, in a heart, or a people, when Jesus Christ is not loved and honored. The same holds true in regard to Jesus and His mother. Where she is not specially loved and honored, where low views are held about her prerogatives, when her spot-less virginity is questioned, where, in short, the mother of God is put on the same level with the mothers of sinners, then is true and sound belief in the nature, person and attributes of her divine son sure to wane in proportion. The main defense of a fortress lies in its outworks. Hence, the Church never wearies in claiming the highest degree of worship compatible with her position as a creature for our Lady. Indeed there is a clear historical connection between the cult of Mary, and the fortunes of the Church. Her victories over error and brute force have been ever followed by fresh devotions, or clearer statements of doctrine, concerning her office and privileges. Development of dogma regarding Jesus from the proclamation of His divinity at Nice to that of His vicar at the Vatican, had its counterpart in the teaching of the Church concerning Mary. And this growth was from within, and not by accretion from without, like a bud gradually ripening into flower and fruit. The great truths of her Immaculate Conception, and glorious Assumption, have sprung from the angel's message and decree of Ephesus, just as branches of a tree come forth from a seedling or sapling. The *"Magnificat"* reveals our Lady to us as the Sermon on the Mount does our Lord.

God's presence and attributes are made known by His works. If He were not reflected in creatures He would be to us an unknown and unknowable God. The starry heavens proclaim His might, and majesty, and wisdom, so does the human soul in a higher degree to those who reflect; if the philosopher's saying is true, "In the world there is nothing great but man. In man there is nothing great but mind," *i. e.*, one power only of the wondrous human soul. Even a building in ruins is proof of an architect and builder; so does fallen man with his body pointing to the earth, and his soul to the skies, show forth the grandeur of his Maker. One thing man has never lost, and that is the perception of higher and better things. This beam of divine light we call the vision of the perfect. It is the *ideal* that ever eludes our grasp, that melts away as we approach it. Everything has its ideal, ever *possible* only, never *actual.* Saints and scholars, poets and artists, are ever straining their gaze after this receding vision. Is it a delusion, or rather is it not a glimpse, a revelation of the plan on which God framed the world and its contents. In this sense we say ideas are the only true, permanent realities. The real is shadowy, transitory, a vain passing show. It does not come up to the ideal, as it exists in the mind of God. Those things only are perfect that express this mind of God. Man is admittedly in the abstract, at least, God's best and highest work. Is there, or can there be, an ideally perfect man, or ideally perfect woman? Is there an absolutely perfect model of humanity—for both sexes? We claim to have the concrete realization—the actual types of the ideal manhood and womanhood of our race in Christ and His blessed mother. Can anyone doubt that amongst men Jesus most perfectly reflects God; and amongst women, Mary. There are no other claimants, nor can there be. For in Jesus "dwelleth all the fulness of the godhead visibly" (Cor. ii, 9) ; and surely she, who was the antithesis of Eve, who was destined to bruise the serpent's head, whose soul "did magnify the Lord," whom the Holy Ghost overshadowed, and whom heaven's messenger saluted as full of grace; and with whom the Lord ever dwelt can aspire to the first, the ideal place amongst women. The two sacred names of Jesus and Mary are ever enter-twined in doctrine and devotion as the two all-perfect specimens of humanity who saved and uplifted our race from the sad state into which Adam and Eve had plunged it. In upholding and defending the name and prerogatives of Mary we are, at the same time, maintaining the claims and attributes of Jesus; inasmuch as it was to fit her to be His mother, that she was so richly dowered by God. She was the golden link uniting the godhead with our

manhood. Rightly do we join with the Church in her praise, saying, "Blessed be the great mother of God, Mary most holy."

II. We may next profitably glance at the thoughts which these
words suggest. Besides the central idea of the divine motherhood,
a title speaking volumes, they remind us that our Lady was blessed,
great and holy, possessing those qualities pre-eminently.

She was blessed far above all other members of her sex. An
angel sent from heaven and a saint, acting under the direct inspi-
ration of the Holy Ghost, used this word, blessed, to express their
admiration of her character and person. It is, in the language it
comes from, where there are two superlative forms for adjectives,
a much stronger expression than in ours. It implies an exceptional
degree of favor, loftiness and excellence. The name "Blessed
Virgin," universally applied to her by friends and foes of the
Church alike, prove how well merited it is. She was blessed because
of the dignity of her office, chosen from among all possible members of her sex as an instrument to give to the world its Redeemer.
God might have come amongst us in some divine way. He might
have woven a vesture of flesh and blood from the elements, as
Adam was fashioned; or as when some of the angels appeared in
human guise. But no! God sent His Son "made of a woman";
and this woman we name Mary, rightly called blessed, as changing
Eve's curse into a source of infinite blessing to our race. She is
the ideal woman, chosen to be the highest expression of the perfection of her sex called, as we have said, to be amongst women,
what Jesus was amongst men. We have but to read the account
of the annunciation, and her own words on occasion of her visit
to St. Elizabeth, as told in the Gospel of St. Luke, to see that God
made her, body and soul, the theater of His marvels. The conviction that to fit her for all this, He made her a being apart, sinless,

stainless, dowered with a radiant and divine beauty, has kept ever deepening in the mind of the Church ever since Gabriel saluted her as "full of grace."

The Most High is represented as addressing this blessed creature of His in the glowing and glittering language of Solomon's love song. They assuredly are blessed whom God favors. Now of her, in words suited to our weakness, He says, "One is my dove, my perfect one is *but* one, she is the *only* one of her mother. The daughters love her and declared her most blessed. Who is she that cometh forth as the morning rising, fair as the moon, bright as the sun" (Cant. vi, 8, 9). And though the most exalted of God's creatures, yet, unlike proud Lucifer and self-seeking Eve, was she the humblest. She recognized whence her greatness came; and for this very reason "He that was mighty regarded the humility of his handmaid, and did great things to her soul."

It is not, therefore, true that in Catholic piety she obscures our Lord, but rather that she enables us to appreciate Him more; just as the beautiful dawn and sunrise prepare us for the full orbed king of day at noon. She is the trophy of God's love, the master piece of His works. The divine gifts and endowments that make her "blessed among women," do but display the wealth of God's treasury. The graces of her person, mind and heart praise, bless and glorify God, the Most High, just as the beauties and wonders of sea, sky and land do.

But not only is our Lady the blessed, she is also the great mother of God. She was truly a great, a grand soul, in the full sense of the term. There was a divine grandeur about her person, her character and her office that entitled her to the first rank amongst the daughters of Eve. To be really great means to have a larger share of God's gifts than others; and who had more than she?

God's gifts are but too often neglected or perverted; but in Mary they "grew and produced fruit an 'hundredfold." They were balanced and adjusted so as to form a perfect whole, making her "the strong and valiant woman, whose value is beyond the bounds of earth," and "terrible" in her greatness "as an army set in array." Character determines greatness, and hers was beyond all praise. How often, alas! is the strength of body, the keenness of intelligence, and force of will that wins for men the title of great, wasted in the temporal and evanescent; or employed in injuring, rather than benefiting, their fallen creatures; but Mary's greatness was true, because her gifts were ever employed in promoting the glory of God and the welfare of men. After all it is God in man that makes man great. Our Lady was truly great, in that "the Lord was with her in all the plenitude of His might and bounty."

She was great in queenly strength. She crushed the old serpent that had subdued the world. She is justly called "the lover of David," "the valiant woman"; and for her share in the Church's conflicts in support of truth and righteousness she has deserved the title of "Our Lady of Victories."

Furthermore she was great in the sense of being gifted with lofty intelligence; for, apart from her own personal powers in this respect, divine wisdom was ever beaming on her soul in undimmed and unclouded splendor. Did not Jesus, the world's true light, "advance" under her fostering care "in wisdom, and age, and grace with God and men"? (Luke ii, 52). The treasures of her knowledge any more than those of her divine Son are not, it is true, enshrined in books, yet the Church enlightened by God does not hesitate to call her the very "seat of wisdom."

Again, she was great in force of will. A truly strong will wherein lies true greatness of character is a will unshaken in its resolve to be conformed to the divine. Eve looked curiously on the glittering serpent, listened, wavered and fell. Mary never parleyed with evil—the antithesis of God's will, and so trampled the foul fiend in the dust. It was God's will, she knew, she should become a mother, and the words, hard to a maiden pledged to virginity: "Be it done to me according to thy word," dropped from her lips. No tenderer or more loving mother ever clasped a babe to breast than she; yet knowing it was the high will of heaven her son should die in untold torments on the Cross, she stood tearless and erect with the sword of grief piercing her brave heart. Strong men quailed, and the band of disciples broke and fled when the powers of hell were let loose against Jesus; but down to the mount where He "bowed his head, and gave up the ghost," "there stood by the Cross of Jesus his mother" (John xix, 25). As I said, what enhanced her greatness in the sight of the Most High, was her humility; but God exalts the humble, and sendeth the rich empty away. Though only a humble "rosebush in Jericho, as spikenard and creeping violet in the woods," "yet was she exalted by her Maker as a cedar in Lebanon."

Finally, our Lady was not only great and blessed, she was holy; and all recognize holiness as the main element of true worth. Men may fail to appreciate it, they may affect to despise it, but at the summit of the gifts that adorn and elevate the soul, holiness stands supreme. It is the divine beauty of the soul, "the pearl of priceless worth, which it were worth a man's while to sell all he has to own." So rare and priceless an endowment is it that souls highly gifted in this respect stand isolated and apart in history. They are the saints of God who stand out like high snowclad mountains, glittering in the sun. Holiness is God in the soul. "The Lord is with thee," was heaven's decree of our Lady's canonization.

Good will and grace are the factors of holiness; and these, as we have seen, she possessed in an eminent degree. Her will never swerved from the straight path of rectitude. It ever pointed to the divine will as unerringly as the needle to the north. The wealth of grace, the talents, the divine capital, so to say, entrusted to her keeping was never lost, buried or wasted, but grew and increased a hundredfold. "Multae filiae congregaverunt divitias, tu supergressa es omnes."

And this wealth of holiness drew God to her, and in the divine plan fitted her to become the mother of His son. She was not a mere passive instrument in the great work of redemption. She was active and free as Eve had been in the fall. Her place in history is, therefore, unique. We all owe her a deep debt of gratitude for the noble part she took with her divine Son in our saving; but she has special claims on the sex of which she was the brightest ornament. If they now share with man the full blessings of Christian liberty—if they are no longer his slaves and toys, but equals and companions—it is to the lowly maiden of Nazareth, who asserted her divine rights before an angel, that they owe it. All worthy men now recognize the claims of wife, daughter and mother to love, reverence and protection—all states of womanhood that our Lady elevated and adorned.

Who would stand by to see them ignored, insulted or despised? If we have dwelt to-day on the greatness and holiness of her whom all generations call blessed, it is to awaken your zeal in defense of her name, and her prerogatives. In defending her you are defending the cause of God, whose best beloved daughter she is, and of Jesus Christ to whom she was a dear and loving mother. As associates of the confraternity of the Holy Name be it your aim and apostolate to correct and repress all low views, false notions and above all, blasphemous reviling of the great mother of God, Mary most holy. And when her praises are sung in church, or her litany and rosary said, join heartily and divinely your fellow worshipers, for you can not think and say too often "Blessed be the great mother of God, Mary most holy."

IX.   "BLESSED BE HER HOLY AND IMMACULATE CONCEPTION"

"Thou art all fair, my beloved, and there is no stain in thee."—Cant. iv, 7.

*SYNOPSIS.—We live in an age of naturalism. There is a ban on the super-
natural  Not only have we to defend free will in man, but in God, too.
Any theory admissible except in faith.  Hence the Immaculate Conception of our Lady and virgin birth of Our Lord so fiercely and persistently
attacked.  God favors, as we see, some creatures more than others.  Why
not His mother according to the flesh?*

*I.   Meaning of dogma defined by Pius IX in 1854.  No more a new
doctrine than divinity of Christ defined at Nice in fourth century.  All
men born in sin.  Our Lady an exception, owing to her dignity and offices;
specially framed to give the world its Saviour.  God could and ought to
have exempted her from general law; therefore, He did.  Argument sound
when looked into.*

*II   Many inklings of this privilege in Scripture (Gen. iii, 15).  If
conceived in sin, and so Satan's slave, how could she crush his head.  Eve,
mother of Cain, came sinless from her Maker's hands; can we think less
worthily of one destined to be the mother of God?*

*Adam born of virginal earth ere blood or sin or putrid corpse defiled
it; so, too, second Adam was born of sinless virgin.  Is addressed as "all
fair" by Him, in whose sight nothing is foul but sin.*

*Lessons.—(1) Hatred of sin.  (2) Love of grace, soul's true wealth.
(3) Zeal in defense of the name, rights and privileges of God and His
mother on earth, the Immaculate Virgin Mary.*

In these days when naturalism is in the ascendant, and everything
in the way of dogma or belief in the supernatural is flouted as
superstition, it behooves us to proclaim more loudly than ever
God's freedom in the realm of law, and His right to create exemp-
tions, or bestow favors where and on whom He pleases.  Miracle
and dogma are surely as reasonable in the sphere of religion as of
nature.  And yet the knowledge of nature, a science, as it is called,
is daily bringing us into touch with wonders as great as those of
the Bible; and truths and theories as hard to bend to as those of
the Catechism.

Never were the doctrines of the sinless origin of our Lady, and
the virgin birth of Our Lord, more fiercely and persistently attacked

than at present, on the ground that God, unlike ourselves, is not free in His own world, but must abide by the arrangements or laws He Himself made for its management. Stripped of the verbiage it is clad in, that is what the denial of miracles comes to.

We are met to-day to defend our Lady in the prerogative of her sinless conception. In doing so we are carrying out the aims and objects of the Society of the Holy Name. Defense of her is defense of God and His Son Jesus Christ—her son, too, in the flesh. Blasphemy and profanity run riot in connection with her name and office, and reflect on her divine Son.

After all, we merely claim that Mary, the mother of Jesus, came forth from her Maker's hands, as Eve, the mother of Cain, did, pure and spotless from sin.

We recall to mind, under the title of her "Immaculate Conception," the first of the "great things" or favors which "He that is mighty" did to the soul of His beloved daughter—the first link in the long chain of graces that made her "all fair" in His sight. In our own day we have had the happiness of seeing the great truth it embodies classed as a solemn dogma of our creed. Long in the land, it at length sprouted forth a full-blown flower on the tree of Catholic belief. Not that it was a new doctrine any more than the truth of Our Lord's divinity was new, though not solemnly defined till the council of Nice, more than three centuries after the first feast of Pentecost. It was always in the mind of the Church. Peter spoke out this mind and set all controversy at rest through the voice of his successor, Pius IX, in 1854.

Like Moses in the desert let us draw reverently near and "see this great sight, why the bush is not burned"—why amidst the flames of sin and concupiscence encircling the human race she alone remains unscathed—why amidst the moral wreck and ruins of humanity she is the only pillar that remains standing. We shall find that God said to her, as King Assuerus to Esther, "The law is not made for thee, but for all others." The dread decree, condemning the descendants of Adam to be born stained with the guilt of *his* sin, has been suspended once, and once only, in favor of this chosen daughter of Israel.

I. As you are aware, dear brethren, we are all, without exception, born into this world infected with the stain of original sin, inherited in the guilt-defiled nature, transmitted downward from Adam, in whom, as St. Paul says, "all have sinned." This takes place in conception, *i. e.,* as soon as human life dawns. The holiest men— even John the Baptist and Jeremias—though cleansed from sin before birth, yet did not escape its stain. Hence we find holy Job exclaiming, "Why hast thou set me opposite to thee" (Job 7), and again the Psalmist, "In sin did my mother conceive me." "Who shall make clean him that is born of unclean seed." Till the purifying waters of Baptism, therefore, flow over us we are sinful in God's sight—shut out from His blessed presence—the bondsmen, in fact, of His arch-enemy, Satan. Now, by our Lady's Immaculate Conception is meant her miraculous preservation by God—who destined her to be His mother in the flesh—the chosen tabernacle wherein for nine months He should dwell—her preservation, I repeat, from incurring this guilt and its consequent penalties—inborn passion and moral feebleness. We believe, and we have both reason and revelation on our side, that as "The glory of children is that of their parents," God preserved, as He *could* and *ought* to have preserved, His mother stainless—that He bade the waters of sin, as of old He did those of the Jordan, stay their onward rush till this new "ark of the covenant" should pass through in safety—we believe that her pure soul, like the dove sent forth from the Ark, was not defiled by the putrid bodies of the dead in a sin-punished world, but returned bright and stainless to the hands of Him who sent it.

II. In Holy Scripture we find many an inkling and intimation of this truth. In the very beginning, before Adam and Eve had left the earthly Paradise a guilty and sin-stricken pair, God promised to raise up a future man and woman—the child and the mother who should undo the work of the serpent and take vengeance on the tempter, Satan. "I will put enmities, he said to the serpent, between thee and the woman, between thy seed and her seed—she shall crush thy head, and thou shalt lie in wait for her heel" (Gen. c, 3). Now, I ask, how could Mary have vanquished or trampled upon the serpent if at any time she had ever been his slave by sin? How could Satan have lain for ages in wait for her heel, if at the very dawn of her being, the very first moment of her existence, he had proudly lorded over her and fettered her soul as he does others in the chain of original guilt? O no! surely the creature who was specially raised up to defeat Satan's craft and restore the bright lustre of her sex, tarnished in Eve's fall could not herself have fallen a victim to Eve's sin—a prey to the seducing wiles of the arch-enemy. "Under the apple tree," says the Holy Ghost, addressing her in the Canticles, "I raised thee up—there was thy mother corrupted." It was underneath this fatal tree that Eve listened complacently to the tempter's voice, and tasted the forbidden fruit. But God in His mercy raised up Mary, a daughter of this same Eve, to defeat Satan's craft and undo its results. Indeed our own inward conviction, our instinct, as it were, of what is right and becoming, forbids the thought of God's permitting her to live even for a moment, and unconsciously, a sin-stained creature. Can we imagine Him looking forward from all eternity with

displeasure, as infinite holiness requires, on one whom He foresaw
He should one day obey and honor and love as a mother. Can we
for a moment think that Mary, the mother of Jesus, had an origin
less worthy than that of Eve, the mother of Cain? Yet Eve came
forth pure, stainless, unsullied from the side of sinless Adam; and
can we think less of the mother of the Incarnate Word?

Adam was formed of the earth whilst the earth was virginal and
pure—of the earth before sin and crime had stained it—or human
blood unjustly shed had flowed upon it, or the bodies of the dead
had entered it. And shall we believe that the earth which God
commanded to bud forth the Saviour, the soil from which Christ
came, was less pure, less virginal, less sinless, than that from which
sinful Adam sprang. No, dear brethren, we can not for a moment
harbor the thought that this "flower from the root of Jesse" had its
beauty ever tarnished by contact with the foul serpent's poisonous
breath. To whom, if not the Blessed Virgin, are addressed the
words of the Holy Ghost in Solomon's mystic song, "Thou art
all fair, my love, and there is no spot or stain in thee." "The Lord
possessed me from the beginning of His ways"—"One is my beloved  .  .  .  the only one of her mother"—to whom is all this
applicable? Not to the Church, often called the spouse of Christ,
for, besides the allegorical sense, they have a literal one—applied to
a person; not certainly the human soul, cleansed by grace; because
stains and spots innumerable cover it. They can only be verified
in the Immaculate Virgin Mary. Now, if the slightest spot of sin
ever rested on her soul she could not be called *all fair* by Him, before whom even the starry heavens are not pure. If a St. Theresa,
a St. Rose of Lima, angels of holiness in the eyes of men; if they
in the light of God's countenance saw themselves as lepers, how
pure and stainless must she have been who ravished the Eternal

with delight.  Worthily does the Church greet her in the words, "Who is she that cometh forth from the desert flowing with delights?"  "Who is she that cometh forth as the morning rising, fair as the moon, bright as the sun."

I know, indeed, it is a law that all men are born sinners—children of wrath—yet where is the law without its exception?  Who can stay the outstretched arm of the Almighty in *mercy* or in *anger?*  It is a law that all men should die, yet Henoch and Elias still live.  It is a law that fire burns, yet the three Israelites cast into the fiery furnace at Babylon walked about unharmed in the midst of the flames hissing and raging around them.  It is a law that water seeks its level, yet the waters of the Red Sea piled themselves mountain-wise to afford a free passage to the fleeing Israelites.  Is the arm of the Lord shortened, or are His mercies diminished.  If He arrested nature's laws in favor of sinners, what may He not have done for His own mother in the flesh?

Now two practical lessons force themselves on the mind from the thoughts suggested by our Lady's sinless origin, her Immaculate Conception, first, to abhor sin, and next to set a high value on the possession of God's grace.  There is only one intrinsic evil absolutely opposed to God, and that is sin.  He pursues it and hates it throughout the ages, wheresoever found, as being radically opposed to His holiness and goodness.  When He would choose a mother to give birth to Him in His human nature, and endow her with gifts and privileges worthy of her high destiny, what did He bestow upon her?  Not exemption from physical pain, from grief, from woe, from poverty, from lowly rank and condition in life.  No!  These are not evils in the strict sense of the terms.  "His ways are not our ways."  The only evil He exempts her from is sin.  This alone is hateful and loathsome in His holy sight.  On the escutcheon of many a noble family - we read the words, "Death rather than dishonor." Now the motto that should be engraven, branded one may say, on the soul of every Christian, and taught us by God's dealings toward His mother, is "Death rather than sin." Any evil, or rather what the world in its shortsightedness calls evil, povery, sickness, neglect, loss of friends and the rest, rather than stain one's ransomed soul by the commission of a wilful and deliberate sin—the infringement of God's binding law in thought, word, deed or omission. We must ever entertain a holy horror of sin, and do our best to abolish its reign in our own hearts, and in those of others. And next to this we must learn from our Lady's spotless holiness to love and value the grace and friendship of Almighty God. What was the secret of our Lady's grandeur that drew the Almighty toward her—that brought the Second Person of the adorable Trinity from heaven to abide within her as in a home and tabernacle. "Many daughters," says the Scripture (Prov. xxxi, 29), "have gathered together riches, thou hast surpassed them all"—not in the riches that men pine for and sigh after—the perishable fleeting goods of earth—no! but the heart's wealth—the riches that never fade—that we can bank for eternal life—the holy grace of God—the jewel of priceless value, for that it is worth while to sell all we have or possess. This is the only treasure worth living and striving for, the only possession that can make us rich in God's holy sight; for by means of this "coin of the kingdom" alone can we "lay hold of eternal life." Wealth, talents, education, rank, prosperity, health—all, in short, that seem to make life worth living— are to the grace of God as the shadow to the substance. Indeed, if they hinder it, or lead away from it, or are not made secondary to it, they are not goods at all, they are positive evils. Evil is that evil does, whatever name it gets. God's favors to our Lady were in the form of grace. In fact wealth and honor, that most people deem essential to happiness in this world, were denied her; or rather in her knowledge of true worth she neither asked for them nor desired them.

We, dear brethren, are by adoption brothers of Christ and children of Mary. She was His last legacy to us from the Cross. St. John represented the Church and us. The highest form of devotion, flattery if your will, is imitation. A man is measured by his ideals. He is lost or saved by them. Low standards ruin souls. Hence God gave us not abstract ideals, but ideals in the flesh—"patterns on the mount"—just to keep us ever looking up and straining forward. This imitation is specially incumbent on us members of the Society of the Holy Name. To sinless and spotless Mary, the holy name of God—the name of her son, and Saviour, ever brought peace, joy and blessing; because ever used by her in prayer and praise. The abuse of the Holy Name must be peculiarly odious to her, knowing as she did the deep reverence due to the name of the Creator. Be it part of our devotion, our homage, our love to her to act up to the spirit of our society in ever defending and reverencing the Holy Name of God—and by extension God's friends, the saints and the queen of saints, the ever blessed Mary. This we must do, not in detached units, but in combination. We must unite to be strong. It is only thus we can show a bold front and hope to prevail against the enemies of God and of His blessed mother.

X. "BLESSED BE THE NAME OF MARY, VIRGIN AND MOTHER"

"Behold a virgin shall conceive and bear a son."—Isaias vii, 14.

*SYNOPSIS.—Introduction.—Maidenhood and maternity ideals of woman-hood. Both realized at one and same time in our Lady. "A virgin shall conceive." Wonder recorded in beginning, middle and end of Holy Writ. War between mother and child of prophecy and dragon of unbelief ever in progress. All must take sides. Duty of Society of Holy Name.*

*I. Let us ponder on force and meaning of ninth in order amongst divine praises Unbelievers would fain persuade the world that our Lady obscures her Son. But answer that true notion of God even, is dis-appearing outside Church, the realm of Mary "Blessed be Name of Mary." Why? Because she undid work of Eve; is Eve's reversal; did for us in redemption what Eve in fall. Is "our Lady" in Church as Christ "Our Lord," is complementary in a certain mysterious sense of Him. This law in her titles, shrines, sanctuaries. Is queen of Church, lady of house of God, in its three realms of earth, purgatory, heaven. Is Esther of people of God Her office gives main value to her name. Is the Miriam of our Exodus*

*II Though wife and mother yet a virgin Consent to become spouse and mother dependent on her presentation of virginity. This seen in "annunciation." Virginity ever prized even in pagan and lustful Rome. Vestals. Weakening of esteem sure mark of decadence Mary remained virgin before, during and after birth of divine Babe Her privilege of motherhood How great. Our Lord's virgin birth postulate of Incar-nation Field of work for members of Society of Holy Name in defend-ing name, honor and prerogative of our Lady*

*Introduction.*—The spotless purity of maidenhood and dignity of maternity are the Christian ideals of womanhood. Whence did they spring? From her who, by special privilege, was at once both virgin and mother. Holy Writ begins and ends with mystic visions of the two central figures of our Creed, the mother and Child—Jesus and Mary. In the third chapter of Genesis the promise is made of a Redeemer to repair the evils of man's fall, in the words spoken to the serpent, the symbol of Satan's evil, "I will put enmities between thee and the woman, and thy seed and her seed; she shall crush thy head" (Gen. iii, 15). The fulfilment of this first prophecy is re-corded in St. John's vision, in the last book of Holy Writ (Apoc. c, xxi), of the woman and her child, persecuted by the great dragon. "A great sign appeared in heaven; a woman clothed with the sun, and the moon under her feet, and on her head a crown of twelve stars. And she brought forth a manchild, who was to rule all nations with an iron rod, and her son was taken up to God. And the dragon was angry against the woman." She had to fly into the desert and be shielded by angels, to protect her own and her son's life. In the very middle of the Bible Isaias the prophet (vii, 14 *et seq.*), on the refusal of Achaz to ask for a miracle, utters the remarkable words I have quoted as my text, "The Lord himself shall give you a sign," *i. e.*, a wonder, a miracle. "Behold a virgin shall conceive and bear a son, and his name shall be called Emmanuel" (Ib. xii, 14). When that virgin offered her Child in the Temple, devout Simeon, taking Him in his arms, prophesied He should be a *Sign* that should be contradicted and that a sword of grief should pierce her own heart. How accurately do all these predictions meet in her, whom we salute as virgin and mother The dragon still pursues her into the desert. The war between his seed (*i. e.,* followers) and hers still goes on. Her son still, after His ascent to God, rules the nations with a rod of iron in the person of His vicar and Church. The raging controversies about the virgin birth and the divine Child going on around us seem an echo of St. John's account of the great *Sign* of the woman and her Babe, told in the twelfth chapter of the Apocalypse. Faith in the virgin mother and her mission is ever at deadly enmity with the dragon of unbelief.

As members of the Society of the Holy Name it is our work and privilege to defend the woman and her Child, who had both to flee into the wilderness from the pursuit of the dragon. It is for us to help to stem the river of profanity and blasphemy that "The serpent cast out of his mouth after the woman, that he might cause her to be carried away by the river" (Ib. xii, 16).

The war between Christendom and its opponents is waged round the actual appearance in history of the virgin mother. Did or did not the eternal God, infinitely removed from matter or all possible contact with carnal lusts, take flesh from a pure and sinless virgin, who, though a mother, yet retained her virginity intact, *before, during* and *after* the birth of her Babe. Did Our Lord come by the usual way of all flesh, or flash from the virgin's womb, like light from a diamond, without affecting the medium through which it passes? Apart from the evidence of Scripture and tradition, to believe that the all pure God should be born into this world as the fruit of carnal conception and in the usual way, is revolting and unthinkable. To hold that any other but an unsullied and virginal mother would be chosen for such a function is tantamount to denying that "the Word was made flesh and dwelt amongst us." Both head and heart gladly join in the prayer we utter in saying, "Blessed be the name of Mary, virgin and mother."

I. Now what value are we to set on these words? It is an old device of Satan to affect surprise that the name of a creature, nay! of a woman, should be solemnly invoked in conjunction with the sacred Name of God. They who, under the plea of reason, revolt from the Church to-day, charge her with idolatry in putting the name and person of Christ on a level with those of God. Their forerunners of the sixteenth century, on the other hand, charged her with obscuring and putting Christ in the background owing to the prominence she gave to the name and cult of Mary. Error is ever inconsistent. The truth is that just as Jesus reveals and magnifies the Godhead, so does Mary heighten and put in true perspective our knowledge of her Son. Jesus, the world's true light, that "enlighteneth every man who cometh into the world," is the Sun of our souls; Mary is, in a manner, like the moon, "the queen of the night"; she reflects His rays. As a matter of fact, it is only among those who worship Jesus and honor His virgin mother that a true and just estimate of the great God, "who made heaven and earth," prevails. Where would the concept of God be if there were no Catholic Church in the world to witness to Him? Outside this kingdom of Christ and realm of Mary the true notion of God is waning and fading away in the world's thought. Its divines and its wise men speak the language of Babel. They are all on the down grade to Pantheism and Atheism. If you doubt what I say, read their books.

No! we praise and bless the name of Mary, virgin and mother, and couple it with that of her divine Son; because in revealing herself as the "woman clad with the sun and the starry diadem around her brow," she at the same time points to God as the source of her perfections. She extols God, not herself, God who raised her up to the dignity she holds, and "did great things to her soul" to fit her for it. We reverence the name of Mary, the woman, our Lady, just as we duly honor the name of "the man Christ," Our Lord. Next to the Holy Name of Jesus, there is none that rouses holier, more tender, or more loving thoughts than that of Mary. The name of Mary reverses the associations coupled with that of Eva, and in its very letters, read backward, gives us the salutation of Ave, with which the angel, voicing a sin-steeped world, hailed her entrance. In her name, therefore, as well as office, she is the antithesis of her who was so intimately connected with our fall. "Good is set against evil, and life against death. Two and two, and one against another" (Ecclus. xxxiii, 15).

She is Eve's counterpart, as Our Lord was Adam's. The Holy

Name of Mary is as closely interwoven with that of Jesus in our redemption as that of Eve with the name of Adam in the fall. In the new kingdom of God we speak of Jesus as "Our Lord" because of the *power,* the *rank,* and the *office* He holds therein; so, too, proportionately do we speak of His mother as "Our Lady." "Her power," like His, "lies in Jerusalem"—the new city of God, "the Church Militant, Suffering and Triumphant, the gates of which God loves more than all the dwellings of Jacob," *i. e.,* the Jewish Church and people. If you want proofs of her *power,* ask her titles, look round the world at her shrines and sanctuaries, read the history of the Church and the lives of the saints, and ask the experience of all who have invoked; and all, without a dissenting voice, will tell you that she is the most powerful of advocates, the Esther of the city of God.

Rank is the place one holds in any social body. Men are grouped according to their merit, their office, and their social standing in the world. In a kingdom, and we give this name to the Church, the society founded by Christ, the highest rank after the king is that of queen. Now Christ is our King—for this He "came into the world," and His kingdom, which "fills the whole earth," has given by unanimous consent the title of queen to His mother. She is called and saluted as such, in its three great realms, earth, purgatory, and heaven. Nor is this a mere empty metaphor. The mind of the Church within her own sphere is the mind of God. She is the organ of His holy spirit. He has put His words into her mouth that "shall not depart from her henceforth now and forever."

Again, in God's kingdom as in every other, function or office determines the worth of one's name. Now the lowest in the kingdom of God is above the highest in all other realms. But what shall we say of the highest possible function that any human being can discharge in relation to the Most High? The nearer a creature is to God the higher it is in the scale of being. The closer we draw to God the more Godlike, the more divine we are. Judge, then, estimate if you can, the worth of the name, and the reverence due to it, of her whose nearness to God was that of a mother to her child. The office discharged by the lowly maiden of Nazareth far transcends any divine commission that we can conceive bestowed on a creature. "Shall not Sion say: A man, yea a man, was born in her, and the highest himself, hath established her" (Ps. lxxxvi, 5). "Glorious things are said of thee, O city of God." The pivot of the glories of Mary, the secret of the almost divine reverence and respect we show to her name, lies in her office of mother of God. "The Word was made flesh" in her sacred person.

Moses, lawgiver and deliverer of the people of God, is one of the chief Scripture types of Christ. So is his sister Miriam a type of our Lady. Born when the cruel edict was in force of drowning all the male children of Israel, she was called Miriam—bitterness of the sea. But when the people of God marched in triumph through the Dead Sea, and thus miraculously escaped their enemies, she sang the song of triumph; and her name was changed to Mary. This same name is given to Our Lady, "Star of the Sea." To storm-tossed souls that sail over the dark waters of life the holy name of Mary is indeed a warning light—a guiding star. In darkness and storm, she heralds the day; she points out the path; leads us to Jesus. There is a secret charm about her name, a name that seems to give light and hope and strength to all who invoke it. Blessed, ever blessed, be the name of Mary, virgin and mother!

II. The creature thus divinely named we proclaim to be a virgin though mother of the Word. Herein lay the great sign or wonder that, according to Isaias, "the Lord himself" gave the world. "Be-

hold a virgin shall conceive and bear a son." Though our Lady's
union with St. Joseph was a true marriage, for he is repeatedly and
truly in Scripture called her husband, yet was it a chaste and spotless union, wherein carnal concupiscence had no lot or part,
like so many unions sealed by vows of chastity that have taken
place in Christian lands since. They recognized that even under
a vow of chastity, two holy souls living in close love and companion-
ship may be truly wed and joined together by that bond which death
only can loosen. It was absolutely necessary that a partner should
be chosen to guard the honor and protect the good name of the
divine mother and Babe, as also to provide for their bodily wants.
It was also doubtless within the scope of God's designs that our
Lady should serve as model and type of all states of womanhood.
During her life she fulfilled the duties and displayed the virtues
that should adorn a woman, whether she be a maiden, a mother, a
wife, or a widow.

So enamored was our Lady of the lily of chastity that she would
have renounced the sublime dignity of mother of God rather than
lose it. It was the angels' assurance that motherhood was compatible with virginity, owing to action of Holy Spirit, which drew
forth her consent, "Be it done unto me according to thy word."
There is no surer mark of degeneracy than lax views about the
honor and chastity of women, or not deeming the virginal state
higher than the conjugal. Even corrupt pagan Rome had its order
of vestal virgins. There is something angelic, not to say divine,
about holy innocence. The very knowledge of the opposite vice,
even when necessary and guiltless, seems to tarnish the mind and
lower the soul's spiritual temperature. Even evil thoughts in this
matter pollute the mind and corrupt the heart.

It would seem an outrage against God to harbor the idea that

He would choose for His mother a being who was not sinless and virginal in body and soul, in mind and in heart. In this respect the teaching of the Church is in harmony with our feelings. In our Lady the honor of virginity was united to the joys and dignity of motherhood. Her maidenhood was preserved as was the burning bush, out of which God spoke to Moses. The budding of Aaron's rod, contrary to all known laws of growth and germination, gives us a vivid picture of Our Lord's virgin birth. The great sign to the nations is the virgin daughter of Israel, who bore a son in whom "the Gentiles should trust." The great kingdom to which all nations are called has for its basis the incarnation of God, the Second Person, in the person of a virgin through the action of the overshadowing spirit. Throughout this work of love, grace and mercy, it is an unshaken doctrine of our faith (C. Lateran can 3) that our Lady remained a stainless virgin *before, during* and *after* the birth of her child—*before,* from the prophecy of Isaias vii, 14, her own vow, and the angels' promise and assurance that it should be respected (Luke i, 34). St. Joseph's fears were allayed by the angel declaring to him that what was conceived in her was of the Holy Ghost (Matt. i, 20). *During birth,* inasmuch as the miracle of the virgin birth lay herein, that Our Lord was born a virgin's son (Isaias vii, 14), just as after death He emerged into the world through a tomb that remained sealed and closed, so did He come as a ray of light through a crystal vase, without violating the integrity of Mary, the inclosed garden of God. Not only have all nations called her blessed, but *"ever a virgin,"* the *"Virgin Mary,"* thus voicing the constant tradition that she remained a virgin *after,* as *before* and *during* the birth of her Babe. To think otherwise would be to dishonor both our Lady and her Son.

To the privilege of perpetual virginity our Lady joins that of motherhood. "Blessed be the name of. Mary, virgin and mother!" We all daily recite the Hail Mary, and gladly salute this great creature, "whose coming brought joy to the whole world," as "Holy Mary Mother of God." Have we ever sifted and winnowed and grasped the thought of the title of *Deipara,* "Mother of God," granted to Mary at Ephesus? Do we ever really bring home to ourselves the truth that the God who rules the skies took flesh and blood, a body and soul, like our own, within the chaste person of her, to defend whose name and honor we have met here to-day. Men wrangle over the virgin birth of Christ. Is it not a necessary postulate of the divine motherhood? Is the title "mother of God" thinkable as applied to any other than a sinless virgin?

When "evil spirits not of God" arose at various times in the history of the Church, and would fain dissolve Christ by various cunning devices against the divinity of His person, the duality of His nature, His true Godhead and manhood, or their union, no more effectual means did the Church adopt than that of tightening the bonds linking mother and Son together. The cult of Our Lord's divinity and its attendant devotions, has ever been accompanied by companion devotions to our Lady. In the new earthly paradise, the Church, Jesus and Mary, the Child and its mother, are as inseparable as were their prototypes in the old, Adam and Eve. The race fell by a woman false to her call, so was it redeemed by a woman ever true to her call. The guilt indeed was man's, as was the price of redemption; but woman, represented by Eve and Mary, had a large share in both.

Here, in the defense of the name and prerogatives of our dear Lady, lies a great field of work for those who stand united in common brotherhood for the defense of the Holy Name. The honor of Mary is the honor of God. To defend her against calumny, insult, profanity and blasphemy is to defend her Son likewise. Ignorance and its offspring, prejudice, are accountable for a great deal of the deplorable abuse of the Holy Names of God, Our Lord, and His blessed mother.

Let us, then, learn and study what our holy religion teaches concerning our Lady and her relations to God. Let us learn how she "magnifies the Lord," and teach others to do so also in their lives. We shall find that he who finds her in the true sense of the term "shall find life and draw salvation from the Lord."

XI.  "BLESSED BE GOD IN HIS ANGELS AND IN HIS SAINTS"

"Thousands of thousands ministered to him, and ten thousand times a hundred thousand stood before him."—Dan. vii, 10

*SYNOPSIS.—Introduction.—God all in all—self-existing, self-sufficing, self-suffering and eternal.   We measured by time, He by eternity.   We shadows, He supreme reality.   Creatures mere dissolving views in time of His eternal thoughts.   A divine element withal in creatures that He seeks and claims; as an artist claims his thought in canvas, book or marble. His glory and bliss independent of creatures.   Relatively, however, they may contribute to them.*

*I.   All creatures praise God materially like instruments in concert. Man and intelligent creatures ought to do so formally, i. e., freely and knowingly.   First duty of man, and an inherent instinct, to praise and bless God.   What else made for, if not mainly this?   Wo to man or angel who fails.   That so many refuse shows forbearance of God and extent of free will.*

*II.   Let us examine meaning of words of tenth amongst Divine Praises.   By the superficial religion deemed superstition; angels and saints imaginary.   But mystery and infinity everywhere.   To whom shall we go for light and leading if not to God?   Error and superstition abound among those who reject Him.   God's image deeply stamped on men and angels.   Chiefly great, and like God, through holiness.   Without it Adam as Lucifer wrecked.*

*Angels; pure, lofty spirits.   Created in grace.   By sort of law all free creatures submitted to test to try their loyalty.   They minister before throne of God and aid mankind.*

*III   Furthermore, God blessed in His saints   Holiness or sanctity creates saints.   No unholy soul can enjoy vision of God   The wicked would be unhappy in heaven.   Saints are heroes and heroines of God's kingdom: our models.   Fix our ideals.   In what holiness consists.   All called to it.   A saint not the growth of a day.*

*Conclusion —Exhort to holiness, sole lasting endowment of soul.*

God is all in all.   He is the source and origin of all being.   Outside His own adorable reality, no influence, motive or cause can weigh with Him, or in any manner determine His acts.   "He hath done all things for himself," not in our sense of selfishness, but because it cannot be otherwise.   He is "from eternity to eternity." We are creatures of time—shadows that flit across the sky.   Strictly speaking, God is the sole reality.   Creatures are but dissolving

views of His eternal thoughts, owing any reality they have to
Him. The artist loves, owns and claims the ideas he expresses in
his works. Poets, painters and sculptors speak of their creations
in poem, picture and marble as their own. There is an element in
them they call theirs. But Almighty God owns, loves and claims all,
because He made all. He seeks in all the divine element He impressed in them. The story of the lost sheep and the prodigal son
is but God trying to restore His shattered masterpiece. From God
creatures came, to God they go. He can not surrender His rights.
They must serve His purpose, for out of Him there is none to
rescue them from His hands. Even fallen angels and bad men,
abusing His gifts of freedom, are but carrying out His plans and
doing His will in spite of themselves. We see a shadow of this in
our own use of noxious plants and animals or of blind and destruc-
tive forces.

I. God is shadowed forth in creatures. All resemble Him in
proportion to the degree of reality bestowed, from dead matter to
highest degree of angel. Their rank in the scale of being depends
on the reality He gave them. Some may deviate from standard
He fixed; all must serve. His essential glory does not depend on
creatures. Relatively and accidentally, however, they may contribute to it. Hence the expression in use among us, *viz.*, to take
away from or promote the honor and glory of God is true in relation to creatures themselves. For the first and main duty of a
rational creature is to praise, bless and give glory to God. The
instinct to do so—religion, in short, is inherent in every soul. It
is only "the fool who says in his heart there is no God." All creatures glorify God—their very existence is an act of praise and
worship, materially speaking. But from men and angels, God expects and requires formal worship, in accordance with their intel-

lectual nature. If not, if they fail to praise, love, and serve God, they are out of tune with the rest of creation. Creation is a hymn to God, and if a single note is missing, the harmony is not complete; and wo to the creatures who, endowed with the divine gifts of intelligence and free will—light in mind to know God and love in heart—consciously fail to worship their Creator. It were better for such if they had never come into being than wilfully refuse to "live to the Lord." What are men and angels for, if not mainly to join in the great concert of praise to the Most High. Sun and moon, stars and light, mountains and hills, kings and all people, young men and maidens, are all invited to praise the name of the Lord (Ps. xlviii). "O all ye works of the Lord, bless the Lord" (Dan. iii, 57). But choice and holy spirits are specially asked thus to glorify God. "The saints shall rejoice in glory, they shall be joyful in their beds. The high praises of God shall be in their mouth. Sing ye to the Lord a new canticle: let His praise be in the church of the saints. Let them praise His name in choir; let them sing to Him with the timbrel and the psaltery" (Ps. cxlix). Hence it is that the Church concludes the divine praises with the solemn invocation: "Blessed be God in His angels and in His saints."

It is a solemn rally cry, to all created intelligences, to join in a great chorus of praise to the Most High. How painful to reflect that so many are silent; nay, that millions of these gifted creatures, whom God made pure, holy, spiritual, use their powers of mind and heart to curse, profane and blaspheme His holy and adorable Name. We shudder when we think that they can do so and live. It is a standing proof of God's mercy and forbearance, as well as the extent to which He has left His creatures free. It is not for us to ask in dismay why so many, on whom God carved so deeply "His own image and likeness," are now numbered among demons and sinners; but rather pray and work so that our lot may be ever cast among the angels and saints.

Not to use words in a vague or indefinite sense, but to grasp well their meaning, let us examine the contents of the last of the divine praises, "Blessed be God in His angels and in His saints."

II. By those who often know least about it, science is said to have dethroned religion, and freed men from its terrors and superstitions. There is a marked tendency nowadays to reject belief in all occult powers and wonders, save those we observe in nature; and deem what we call the whole supernatural order as void of truth and reality, as witchcraft. By those who regard one world at a time as enough, angels and saints and demons are therefore looked at much in the same light as giants and fairies. But this way of looking at things is mere superficial flippancy or crude materialism. Religion is too deep a need of mind and heart.

Never did seriously reflecting men feel more the need of God. Knowledge shows us, brings home to us, the Infinite in every leaf and flower. The seen has its roots in the unseen. The invisible and the infinite are the only explanation of the finite and the visible. Hence the ever increasing interest in religion in the thinking world and the growth of new forms of it. We live in an atmosphere electric with mystery. We are in the grip of unseen powers not ourselves. Where are we to go for light and guidance. There is cold comfort outside belief in the "one true living God, and Jesus Christ, whom He has sent." Cults of all sorts abound, for the instinct that prompts man to worship is too strong to be resisted, but all can not be true or lawful any more than divergent and opposing theories in science. If men will not believe in the angels and saints of the kingdom of God, they will turn to the spirits, bad and good, that are offered them in spiritualism, or the many other

quasi-scientific superstitions of the day. A scorner of truth falls a
victim to error. Reverence, praise and worship denied to the
Holy Name of the true God, end in profanity and blasphemy
against it.

But to come back to the subject of angels and saints. The
divine element is more vividly expressed and revealed in them than
in other creatures. God sees more of Himself in them than in
others. All intelligent beings reflect God, it is true, but holiness is
more Godlike than knowledge. Intellectual ability, indeed, if it
leads not to holiness, is more hurtful than otherwise, as we see
in demons and wicked men. God is goodness without limitation or
qualification. The earth was a dead, inert mass till life appeared on
it and culminated in intelligent life. One man was master of the
whole earth, and immeasurably greater and more important than it.
Indeed its ownership did not satisfy him, because he so reflected
God in mind and heart that God alone could fill them. When
he lost holiness, when he ceased to be a saint, God faded away from
his soul, and he became a wretch, but still great and noble as a
ruin.

Now it would be absurd to think that God's creative energy in
the world of intelligence stopped short at man—a creature half
matter, half spirit. The soul of man is great, but a pure angelic
spirit is by nature greater. In this, revelation and faith quite accord
with reason in making known the existence of angels, pure and
lofty spirits, dowered with intelligence, free will, and other powers
higher than our own. Their existence is repeatedly alluded to in
holy Scripture, though often erroneously asserted that the Jews
borrowed their ideas of angels from Greek and Chaldean sources.
Allusion is made to them even before the captivity of Babylon.
Indeed the doctrine about angels forms part of the primitive tra-

dition from whatsoever source it came (Gen. xx, 11; Exod. iii, 2; Numb. xxii, 22; Isaias liii, 9).

They are not emanations of God, but creatures, and as such, subject to limitations. Though endowed with grace, they were not at first in the enjoyment of the beatific vision, a thing incompatible with sin. On the contrary, it is of faith that a large number fell or lapsed from grace (Matt. xxv, 41; Luke x, 18; II Pet. ii, 4; Apoc. xii, 7, 8). It would seem to be a divine law that every intellectual creature must be submitted to a test or trial. All, whether men or angels, must win their crowns; and pass through the fiery ordeal of temptation.

They must first use their gift of freedom in choosing or selecting ing God ere He chooses them. It is generally believed that one-third of their number fell into some form of the sin of intellectual pride For one may rebel against authority by stubbornness of mind as by revolt of will, though sin is ultimately a product of will. There is a tradition that the souls of the elect are destined to fill the depleted ranks of the angels.

Be this as it may, the good angels rallying around their leader, St. Michael, to the cry of *"Quis sicut Deus"* are now confirmed in grace, ever beholding the face of "their father who is in heaven."

They form the ranks of the good angels, who are put before us as ministering before the throne of God and employed in guiding, helping and guarding us poor, weak, spiritually helpless human beings.

There is a great deal of interesting speculation among sacred writers as to the number, classes, powers and functions of angels. As there is order, rank and development in all God's creations, so must there be among those blessed spirits that come so near to Him; but it is almost idle to dogmatize in the matter. What we

know for certain is that they ever give praise, honor and glory to
Almighty God.  They use their marvelous and varied activities of
intelligence and will in the service of God and the contemplation of
His attributes.  Even in this world of shadows, where the wisest
barely grasp the surface of things, we know what floods of delight
pass over the soul in the exercise of our mental powers, to say
nothing of the pleasures of sense and the ravishing ecstasies of
love; what, then, will the life and joy of angels be in the gaze of
God—the great sea of truth, light and love, whence all things
sprang.  Their whole beings burst forth into songs of love, wonder
and praise.  "And all the angels stood round about the throne . . .
and they adored God, saying, Amen.  Benediction and glory and
wisdom and thanksgiving, honor and power and strength to our
God forever and ever" (Apoc. vii, 11, 12).

II.  Furthermore, we pray that God may be blessed not only in
His angels, but in His saints.  It is holiness that makes a saint.
God is essentially holy; and no unholy soul can live, much less be
happy, in His company.  Heaven is the vision of God—a special
mode of His presence.  In the new Jerusalem, or Paradise, it is
said (Apoc. xxi, 22, 23) that there is no temple, "For the Lord
God Almighty is the temple thereof, and the Lamb.  And the city
hath no need of the sun nor of the moon to shine in it.  For the
glory of God hath enlightened it, and the Lamb is the lamp thereof."
The light of God's countenance makes heaven, just as its absence
is essentially hell.  By the very nature of sanctity—*i. e.,* by the very
state of their souls—the saints are blessed in the vision of God and
sinners are unhappy and accursed.  Pitch is, and remains, black,
though all the suns in the sky were to shine upon it; and snow
is white under a single ray.  Hence Our Lord's exhortation "Be
ye holy as I am holy," "Be ye perfect (*i. e.,* holy) as my heavenly

Father is perfect." The evolution of saints, it may be said with truth, is the object of all creation. All things change and pass away, the very stars will be blotted out. But behold, says the Almighty, I create new heavens and a new earth, and what is this but the kingdom of the saints, that will endure forever. "I create Jerusalem a rejoicing, and her people a joy." Hence though God is wonderful in all His works—even a flower revealing a world of wonders to "searchers after truth," yet God is said to be *admirable* in His saints, *"Admirabilis Deus in sanctis suis."*

The soul of the kingdom of God is holiness. They are of the kingdom who are holy, even though not of it bodily. From stones even God can raise up children to Abraham. When Christ would form His kingdom and raise up an acceptable people, He took of every class. His servants were ordered to scour the highways and byways, the lanes and the alleys of life, and bring halt, and blind, and maimed, as guests to the royal supper. So in His kingdom, the Church, to-day. The material for saints is as diverse as may be. The grace of God, co-operating with free will, is all that is required. Simple fishermen, like Peter and Andrew, or learned and cultured scribes, of the type of St. Paul and St. Luke, afford fitting stones to be built into the heavenly Jerusalem.

In the infant Church all its members were called saints, as the good and holy so far outnumbered the bad as to give their name to the whole. In early ages, too, the title was bestowed by *acclamation;* unerring popular instinct fastening on those in whom the spirit of God shone pre-eminently. Nowadays those specially remarkable for high personal virtue and eminent services to religion are canonized by regular form and procedure, through the three stages of veneration, beatification and canonization. Saints are the heroes and heroines of God's kingdom. In fighting the good fight, conquering self, overcoming God's enemies, the world, the flesh and the devil they display a bravery and persistence far above the common.

Besides this, there are in the minds and hearts of the saints lights, instincts, discernments and intuitions that transcend those of people who walk on the common level. A person on a hilltop, a church spire, or even raised on another's shoulders, sees further afield than those below. So with the saints. They are rare servants of God, whom He raises up in all ages, to show how far human nature can attain to the likeness of His Son. They are angels in disguise, whom we would fain salute with divine honor, were we not assured that they are mortals like ourselves. Indeed, we rightly call them angels in the flesh, for in them the carnal element of our nature holds no sway. They fix our ideals. They are modeled so perfectly on Our Lord and His blessed Mother, that they keep our gaze ever raised upward. Looking up to sun, moon and stars in the sky is like lifting our eyes to Christ, the blessed Virgin, the saints in the spiritual firmament. We know we can not reach or follow them; but they enlighten, guide and direct our paths withal. The ideal in holiness, as in art, is everything; even though unattainable. Now, it is in all special manner, in these holy souls, whether in the Church Militant on earth, Suffering in Purgatory, or Triumphant in Heaven, that God is blessed, praised and magnified. We may even solemnly and publicly invoke in prayer those declared to have won their crowns in heaven. They are the special friends and favorites of the Most High. He sees more of Himself reflected in them than in others. Holiness is the highest endowment of a creature because rendering them more God-like. Hence, as God "draws all to Himself, because as far as it is real it is Himself shadowing." Holiness attracts God, whilst wickedness repels Him.

Not that He hates the sinner; but He sees no image of Himself there. The light or vision of God is heaven to the saints, hell to sinners. They can not, dare not, look on the all-holy God and live. Heaven, if allowed to enter, would be hell to them. The "vision of the lamb" would torment them like the devils in Scripture, they would say to Christ "Let us alone, what have we to do with thee." As we see even in this world, piety is loathsome to the unholy and uncovenanted. The holiness of the saint is gall and wormwood to the sinner. Cain and Abel are ever at war. The dragon never ceases to pursue the woman and her seed, i. e., the Church and the elect. For the same reason whilst the name of God is blessed, praised and revered by angels and saints, it is loathed, profaned and blasphemed by devils and bad men.

We must all then join hands with the saints. Nay, more, though the world we live in "is seated in wickedness," we must yet in a measure be saints, i. e., holy. It is an irreversible law that holiness is a state of soul without which we shall never see God, i. e., be saved. By nature and habit we may be weak, corrupt, unholy, yet are we enjoined, one and all, to become "new creatures" in Christ. To be holy is more than to feel holy. To be a saint is to have God's grace and live unspotted from the world. It is to shun and hate, in the manner prescribed by God's law, God's enemies, the world, the flesh and the devil. It is to be dead to sin and alive to God. This state of heavenly mindedness, or holiness, is not acquired in a day. It is a frame of mind, a set of tastes, views and habits that are often the work of self-sacrifice of a long life. A saint no more than a scholar is the growth of a day. Mushrooms grow in a night, but oaks and cedars take centuries. The only hope for habitual sinners is that it is never too late to mend, and that perhaps there are more miracles in the kingdom of grace than in the kingdom of nature.

One thing is certain: if we would be saints in heaven we must be saints on earth. Let us keep this thought before us, when we say devoutly with the Church: "Blessed be God in His angels and in His saints."

XII.  "GLORY BE TO THE FATHER AND TO THE SON AND TO THE
HOLY GHOST"

"And there are three who give testimony in heaven, the Father, the Word,
and the Holy Ghost.  And these three are one."—I John v, 8.

*SYNOPSIS.—The divine praises seem incomplete without the "Gloria Patri,"
etc., which, usually, either ends or enters into all the public prayers of
the Church  Hence fitting subject for concluding discourse  Doxology
dates back to earliest times—probably a protest against Arianism.  God
triune.  Should be the main note of life, as glory of God, one in three, is
main end of creation*
    *I.  Mystery of Trinity; challenge to rationalism, at threshold of
faith.  Fundamental truth.  Though incomprehensible, yet illumines mind
and heart.  No strain on reason; tones and elevates  All life a web of
mystery; much more the inner life of God*
    *What reason teaches in natural theology, about nature and at-
tributes of God, apparently impossible and contradictory to our experience; yet necessary truths.  Need we wonder, then, that the truths of
faith are beyond our grasp.*
    *II.  Not a barren dogma; but fruitful in practical application and
results.  How so*
    *The "Gloria Patri" best expresses what should be our attitude, in
mind and heart, toward Almighty God  Is the prayer of a multitude
God's love of united prayer and praise.*
    *Exhortation thereto.*

*Introduction.*—By way of conclusion to our course of instruction
on the divine praises, I choose as subject the minor doxology, as
it is termed, "Glory be to the Father and to the Son and to the Holy
Ghost."  Reflections on the Holy Name would appear incomplete
without special reference to the Father and the Holy Ghost in the
blessed and adorable Trinity.  In the great work of praising God no
form of prayer is more appropriate or more frequently used than
the "Gloria Patri," etc.  It is, in fact, a short summary of the whole
duty of prayer and praise.  In its present form it dates quite as far
back as the fourth century, and was first appended to the Psalms
by Pope Damascus.  At present in the divine office, in the Rosary,

in the administration of the Sacraments and sacramentals, this solemn and stately prayer is ever heard. And rightly so, for belief in and devotion to the Holy Trinity interpenetrates Catholic life, thought, and worship. The God, whom we are born to love, serve, and praise, is a triune God.

Moreover, the frequent and fervent utterance of this prayer is not only a short method of rendering to Almighty God the daily tribute of prayer and praise we owe Him; but is also a telling act of reparation for the many outrages committed against the Holy Name. They who ignore God's name, or worse still, they who abuse it by cursing, swearing, or blasphemy, take away from the praise and glory due to God the Father, God the Son, and God the Holy Ghost. To express and uphold this praise and glory should be our main effort and honor in life. The Church is our model in this respect, ever beginning her prayers and actions with the solemn invocation of the Trinity in the sign of the Cross, and ending with the doxology.

I.   The truth expressed in the word Trinity, *viz.*, one God in three distinct persons, is a direct challenge to rationalism in every shape and form. It is one of the great truths that must be known and believed by all, under pain of sin, unless excused by invincible ignorance; and which is ever expressly proposed to those seeking admittance into the Church. It thus requires unconditional surrender of private judgment at the very threshold of faith.   Not that the mystery of one God in three persons is subversive of reason, or even puts an undue strain upon it.   All that we can say against it is that it can neither be proved nor disproved by the light of unaided human intelligence.   Though faith's first and hardest trial, yet once embraced it floods the mind with light and the heart with peace, and helps us somewhat to unravel the web of mystery around us, in nature without, and in our own minds within. Man's fitting attitude to this great truth is well expressed by St. Paul in the epistle read on Trinity Sunday: "O the depth of the riches of the wisdom and of the knowledge of God! How incomprehensible are his judgments, and how unsearchable his ways" (Rom. xi, 33). The mystery of the Trinity should engender reverent awe, not doubt or unbelief. True, it is unfathomable; but so is all mystery, and, as I said, mystery is no strain on reason. Reason itself is immersed in mystery. The world we live in teems with it. Life, in even its lowest forms, is a web of mystery. If, then, facts palpable to sense are, in their essence, origin and bearing, mysterious and impervious to reason, can we expect the inner life of God to be within the comprehension of our puny understandings? The very angels and saints in the flood of the "light of His countenance" can but veil their faces and repeat, "Holy, holy, holy, Lord God of Sabaoth, heaven and earth are filled with thy glory." Finite mind can not grasp the infinite. Were God to unveil the mystery of His unity of nature in trinity of Persons to the utmost capacity of our minds, we should just be as far from fully understanding it as ever.

Indeed, the delight of the blessed, in the vision of bliss, springs from this impossibility of ever exhausting the knowledge of God. There is no monotony, but ever-increasing wonder, in this knowledge. This truth is shadowed by our incapacity to understand God's works on earth. There is a fascination in our very ignorance of them. The delight of great learning is to realize how very little we know and how much remains to master. This very weakness of mental vision does but spur to deeper inquiry. No true botanist or entymologist will say he knows all that can be known about a flower or a fly. Is it wisdom or shallowness, then, to turn sceptic or agnostic because God has not revealed himself more fully in reason

and faith? Look at his footprints in nature. How clean and wonderful, yet how dark and incomprehensible, they all are! The field
of knowledge is broad and long. The wise of all times ever have
been, and ever are, busy in mapping it out, and naming and classify-
ing its contents. All, whether they are physicists penetrating into
the inmost recesses of matter, following and tracing it down to its
ultimate atoms or molecules, or whether they are metaphysicians,
who take the subject up where the others leave off, own, after rang-
ing the whole realm of speculation, that their researches, even in
matter, end in mystery, and that an impenetrable veil hides the inner
nature of the most common things that we daily see, touch and
taste. How much more true is this, in the unseen, though not less
real, world of spirit. All knowledge, howsoever pursued, leads to
God, whatever name men may give Him. He is behind the veil
of mystery, the first beginning and last end of all created things.

When people, therefore, are tempted to complain that the Trinity
and other truths of religion weigh too heavily on the mind, they
should remember that the how, why and wherefore of the visible
and palpable facts of daily experience are wrapped up in secrecy
just as impenetrable. The wonders of plant and animal life, the
marvels of sound, color, light, heat, gravitation and electricity, the
fact that two such radically opposite substances as soul and body, one
a living force, that feels, thinks and wills, the other, woven by this
vital power out of dead matter, work so harmoniously together for a
common purpose, is all, except on the surface, profoundly mysterious. More than half our energies of mind and body are spent in
procuring food and drink, yet who reflects on the mystery of their
change into blood, and this again into living tissue, forming bone,
muscle, nerve or skin, as required?

Faith makes known to us the being of one God in three distinct

Persons, yet what unaided reason compels us to believe about the nature and attributes of God is just as apparently unthinkable. Even the shallowest mind is forced by the laws of thought to own that there can be no endless chain of cause and effect. Reason must finally rest in some uncaused and self-existing being, who ever *is* and who came from no other—some mighty changeless spirit, weaving about Him in this vast world an *ever changing* web of beings we call "creatures of time," and which are but the marks, traces, footprints of the Eternal Presence, in whom "we all live, move and have our being." But who can gauge the meaning of the words *eternal, necessary, self-existing*? They run counter to our experience. They seem contradictory, incredible. Withal reason compels belief in the existence of a being who has all these attributes. He must be without a beginning, eternal. If anything exists at all, some being must always have been from all eternity to start it. There is no way out. God or the world is eternal, self-existent, necessary. And yet it is the height of unreason to say the world or anything in it made itself. The marks of time, dependence, a beginning, and an end, are stamped in it. The universe points to an eternal, self-existing intelligence from which all things sprang. "Thou, O Lord, hast created us, and not we ourselves." "The invisible things of him," *i. e.,* His mysterious attributes, "are clearly seen" in reason, "being understood by the things that are made" (Rom. i, 20). The Apostle goes on to show how the mind is forced by a process of reasoning, easy to the rudest, to admit the necessity of a Supreme Being—a Being standing to us in the relation of judge, as proved by conscience and our knowledge of the moral law. "Their conscience bearing witness to them and their thoughts accusing or defending" (Rom. ii, 15).

Faith completes and perfects the knowledge of God, furnished by reason. Unaided reason tells us nothing of the inner life of God; whereas faith instructs us that in the bosom of the one eternal, infinite, self-existing Godhead there is a unity of nature and trinity of Persons—each of which has distinct personal relations to each other and to us. It informs us that there is one God in three distinct Persons, that the Father is God, the Son is God and the Holy Ghost is God, and yet that there are not three Gods, but only one God. In the Father is displayed to creatures the power, in the Son the wisdom, and in the Holy Ghost, the love of God. Every time we devoutly say, "Glory be to the Father and to the Son and to the Holy Ghost," we solemnly adore and profess our belief in this triune God.

Though the praise of the blessed Trinity is now on "the lips of babes and sucklings," yet it took three centuries of incessant war against ever-recurring heresies to root this great truth firmly in the mind and conscience of the Church. The decrees of Nice closed the controversy, as far as the Church was concerned; but it keeps ever reappearing in various forms outside her fold. Indeed, denial of the Trinity, or wrong views about it, or some kindred truths linked to it, are in some way or other the standing theological errors of the day.

The great truth of the Trinity dawned early on the Jewish mind, as we shall see; neither was it altogether unknown to the Gentiles, to such an extent, indeed, that many assert St. John to have learned part, at least, of his sublime outburst about the Divinity of the Word, the Second Person of the Trinity, from Greek sources of thought. Though only emerging clearly into light in Our Lord's day, yet it dimly cast its shadow in the older revelation, as may be learned from reference to such texts as Gen. i, 26; iii, 22; xi, 7; Ps. xxxvii, 6, and various others, where there is a vague indication of plurality of functions, or persons, in the one concept of God. Excessive light may, in some cases, dazzle and blind rather than illumine. To rude, untrained minds, in the childhood of the race, or in an age seething with idolatry, there was danger in fulness of light in such a subject as the Trinity. The truth it involves, though not the word itself, was first clearly taught in the New Testament. In Matthew xxvii, 19, Our Lord sends forth His disciples to teach all nations, "Baptizing them in the name of the Father and of the Son and of the Holy Ghost." In His promise of the Paraclete (John xiv, 16); at His Baptism by John (Matt. iii, 16, 17), and in the triple testimony quoted in I John v, 7, this mystery is clearly set forth. These statements, together with the other hints and symbols on the subject, formed the germ of the doctrine of the Trinity that developed into full expression in the creeds and writings of the fathers, as well as in the devotions of the Church. We may say, indeed, that all Catholic doctrine, practise, and devotion branch off from, or circle round, the great central truth of one God in three Persons. Over and above the special feast dedicated to the cult of the Trinity, every Sunday is set apart to honor this mystery.

Instances occur in nature wherein unity and trinity meet and combine, thus shadowing forth the mystery of one God in three divine persons. The commonest form of division of a whole, real or logical, is usually threefold. The mind seems to fall into this way of viewing things almost by instinct. Our own souls bear the impress of this mystery in branching out into three distinct powers, the memory, the will, and the understanding. Life is threefold, vegetable, sensitive and rational. Again, matter exists under three forms or states, the solid, the liquid, and the gaseous. In each order of plant we find seed, stalk and flower. Dimension likewise is threefold, length, breadth and thickness. So, too, is the relation of time, into present, past and future. In the family we find unity in the triple relation of father, mother and child. These and many others, though apparently casual, are yet singular coincidences.

II. It is often objected that the dogma of the Trinity, which we glorify in the doxology, is a hard, unintelligible puzzle, quite barren of all practical effect on life or conduct. The same objection might be made to more than half the truths that make up the sum of human knowledge. As a matter of fact, no truth, howsoever speculative, is barren of effect, least of all the Trinity. Apart from the light it throws on the life, nature and attributes of Almighty God—the highest and most excellent subject of thought, it is of intense personal interest to each one of us, and profoundly affects our destiny for time and eternity. For one thing it lets us know the awful nature of sin, to save from which one of the three divine Persons chose to suffer in the flesh. And, again, can that truth be called barren and fruitless which lets us know with unerring certainty that we have a Father in heaven who created us, His divine Son who redeemed us, and the Holy Ghost who sanctifies us and breathes into us the breath of spiritual life? The first inkling of the Trinity in the Old Testament was given at the creation of man when God breathed into the body prepared to receive it a rational soul—a pure, innocent, sinless spirit—saying in His triple personality, "Let *us* make man to our own image and likeness." And when this divine image, blurred and marred and well nigh effaced by sin, is restored again in holy Baptism, the magic change is effected through a rite administered "in the name of the Father and of the Son and of the Holy Ghost."

Our redemption is complete when the image of God, shattered in the fall, is restored, and man stands up again before his God remade in His image and likeness. The restoration of a soul to grace on the part of Almighty God is an act of creation repeated. In the words of St Paul, we become "new creatures in Christ Jesus." Now to effect this restoration of fallen man, all three divine Persons of the Trinity co-operate. The Father aids in drawing us to seek the grace we lost. "No one cometh to Christ to have the image of God restored" unless the Father draweth him. The Son furnishes us with grace in the Sacraments He has instituted, the sacred fountains and furnaces wherein this restoration is effected. The Holy Ghost, the spirit of order and life, keeps alive the spark of divine life and grace—indispensable condition for the maintenance of the divine image in our soul.

And when the triune God has restored His image and again made our souls like to Him in the divine cast given to our mind, will and affection, when we are thus made sons of God by adoption, are welcomed back to our Father's house and receive the robe of grace, the indispensable wedding garb, then, and not till then, can we sit down in peace and joy at the King's table and unite with the saints and angels in singing with heart and voice, "Glory be to the Father and to the Son and to the Holy Ghost."

This must be the trend of our lives. To voice the praise of God, to honor duly His Holy Name, to sing worthily the divine praises is the highest function of a creature. To urge you to it is the purpose of what we now say, and have hitherto said, on the subject of the doxology and the divine praises. The worship of God, adoration of our triune Creator, in spirit and truth, must be the main purpose of intelligent life. God can have had no other in making us, and it should be ours. It is folly and waste of time to argue against it. If we are immortal spirits in perishable bodies, the interests of the soul and of eternity, not those of the body and of time, must chiefly concern us. "To seek first the glory of God," to render due homage in belief and conduct to Father, Son and Holy Ghost, is, in the long run, the highest aim, as it is the highest wisdom, and interest of man.

Apart from this, surely a feeling of awe, mingled with the deepest love and respect, must sweep over our souls when we reflect on the overwhelming mystery of the Trinity—that vast ocean of divine life, uncaused, self-existing, self-sufficing, dwelling from all eternity "in light inaccessible" before the sun or stars shone in the sky. Before mind or matter, man or angel saw the light, God, one in three, was, is, and ever will be. And just to think that we sinful creatures are privileged to know God, to name Him, to love, serve and praise Him forever. Who, revolving these thoughts in his mind, will dare to say that the time is wasted which is spent in praising and blessing the Father who created us, the Son who redeemed us, the Holy Ghost who sanctifies us? Were we logical and consistent with our beliefs our entire lives should virtually be a perpetual doxology, a life-long repetition in mind, heart and voice of "Glory be to the Father and to the Son and to the Holy Ghost."

To none do these words apply more than to us whose special mission it is to defend among men the Holy Name of God, and suppress, as far as in us lies, its abuse. To us the Trinity and the Holy Name of God are one and the same thing. The use of those sacred names should be ever sacred and confined, as in the doxology, to prayer and praise.

But remember, the doxology is essentially a many-tongued prayer. It is the exulting cry and call to God of a multitude. Though each soul is individually distinct and personally responsible, yet God made us, and meant us, to live and work and pray in groups. We are elements of one great humanity, called as a whole to glorify God. Our strength lies in the unity of common brotherhood. We shrivel in isolation. God loves multitude. Nothing stands alone. He has planted us in families, tribes and nations. "Where two or three are joined together in his name there is he in the midst of them." His Church is one body, meant to gather in all nations of the earth "to praise the name of the Lord." However tunefully an individual may sing, yet if it does not blend into harmony with the whole choir, it is but as discord before the Lord. Hence, the various nations, orders, congregations, brotherhoods of the Church, are but parts of a great whole, tuned to praise and worship God in harmony. Howsoever divided in other respects, yet her authority, her teaching, her Sacraments and sacrifice are great blending and incorporating forces divinely inforcing unity. Wo to any man, or body of men, that "divides Christ." Wo even to the solitary Catholic who does not keep in bodily union with those who believe in and adore the Father, Son and Holy Ghost.

Never, therefore, choose, of your own accord to live in a place where you can not join your fellow Catholics in the divinely established praise and service of the Trinity. The new Jerusalem is a city of peace, a commonwealth of concord, both above and below.

Bear all this in mind in your mission of spreading devotion to the Holy Name. God is *our* Father, *our* Redeemer, *our* Saviour, not *mine* exclusively, therefore must we draw tightly together in the bonds of holy brotherhood, pray *together* and *for* one another, work together and so be saved together in and through the Father, Son and Holy Ghost, to whom be honor, praise and glory now and forever.

Milton Keynes UK
Ingram Content Group UK Ltd.
UKHW021938280124
436871UK00003B/7